PRAISE FOR AFA PITTS AND
The ABCs of Flipping

If you watch TV, home improvement shows rank at the top, and they always conclude with a happy ending. But they never show the entire process that goes into flipping homes.

Although flipping presents unlimited possibilities for huge profits now and into the future, the flipper must be fluent in the entire process—from initially researching the market through the intricacies of completing the final sale. This book addresses all the necessary steps to make you successful.

Dr. Afa Pitts, with her extensive background in medicine, knows how to pay attention to detail. She presents in-depth instructions in a proven educational approach, using the alphabet to arrange chapters in a way that can be fun, easily absorbed, and retained. Just remember your ABCs.

This book is an absolute necessity for anyone interested in flipping houses and even those who are interested in purchasing flipped homes. This is where you need to start. I highly recommend it.

—Dr. Paul J. Pavlik
CEO and Founder, Tracker Enterprises, Inc.

An innovative approach to flipping in today's uncertain real estate market with just the right amount of attention on planning and execution to get you out of your head and into investing. Afa Pitts reflects on her lessons and successes, holding your hand through the process of succeeding in both flipping and life.

—Shenoah Grove
Founder, Texas REIAS

Afa Pitts combines her competitive spirit, passion for winning, engaging leadership energy, focus on quality, and overall personal programming for success to develop and articulate a proven strategy to successful real estate flipping. This eye-opening, common-sense, and engaging read weaves the perfect balance of proven success with a reliable and easy to follow roadmap. An absolute must read for the novice and expert real-estate investor.

—Marie Alvarado
Director of Operations, U.S. Congressman John R. Carter

THE ABCs OF FLIPPING

AFA PITTS, MD™

THE ABCs OF FLIPPING

YOUR GUIDE TO BUYING, REHABBING, AND SELLING HOUSES

Advantage | Books

Published by Advantage, Charleston, South Carolina.
Member of Advantage Media.

ADVANTAGE is a registered trademark, and the Advantage colophon is a trademark of Advantage Media Group, Inc.

Printed in the United States of America.

10 9 8 7 6 5 4 3 2 1

ISBN: 978-1-64225-776-2 (Paperback)
ISBN: 978-1-64225-775-5 (e-book)

LCCN: 2023901623

Book design by Analisa Smith.

Advantage Media helps busy entrepreneurs, CEOs, and leaders write and publish a book to grow their business and become the authority in their field. Advantage authors comprise an exclusive community of industry professionals, idea-makers, and thought leaders. Do you have a book idea or manuscript for consideration? We would love to hear from you at **AdvantageMedia.com**.

To my parents,
for raising me to believe that anything was possible

To my husband,
for making everything possible

To my kids,
for the amazing happiness they bring me every day

CONTENTS

INTRODUCTION

House flipping has never been more enticing and exciting. The popularity of various reality shows based around flipping and design has skyrocketed. Who doesn't love to see those transformative "befores" and "afters"? Watching a young couple find the starter town house of their dreams or a family find their perfect forever home pulls us all in emotionally. These shows spur the creative mind with what is possible in a house redesign or flip.

Knocking down walls, building custom closets, creating a new kitchen, painting the exterior, and landscaping—some homes need a little work, and some are gutted from top to bottom. The best designers and flippers are visionary and see the potential of a house with a little (or a lot of) TLC.

For me personally, house flipping not only provided an excellent income and a pathway to business investment, but it also afforded me the ability to both help people and have a creative career that isn't just a nine-to-five job. I've since moved on to investing in businesses—but it all started with house flipping. I knew even as a medical doctor that business was something I was both interested in and excelled at.

Average profits for house flips can be between $30,000 and $60,000, depending on the number of repairs needed.[1] However, certain markets and certain price points can deliver much higher profits. Even with having investments across the country, I really like and liked working in Texas, where the market is considered hot (as of this writing, but markets are rapidly changing—and house flippers should know you can expect a bumpy ride sometimes). Hot markets, though, have limited inventory, since everything gets snapped up so quickly—so a house flipper is going to want to be as networked and connected to the community and contacts in that market as possible. But there has never been a more exciting time to be in the flipping business.

My background as a medical doctor always combined my compassionate nature with my analytical side. That same duality was part of my approach to flipping and investment. When I moved to the United States—confronted with red tape of transferring my medical license and never wanting to be idle—I was intrigued by the idea of pursuing business opportunities. I loved seeing my vision for a house come alive. I was inspired by the idea of finding a run-down house, a property that was outdated or needed some attention and TLC, and transforming it for a new, young family or someone who wanted to be in that neighborhood but lacked the skills and concepts to transform the house themselves. Because of my methods, API Inc. (https://apinvestments.us) offered quality homes with attractive finishes and the look home buyers seek. I often heard (and still hear) from buyers even two years later or more: "Oh, we still love everything about the house. Whenever we have company, everyone just adores our home." I stand behind our work, our homes, our product. Those calls made me feel good about my visions for those homes.

Another aspect I loved about finding people the home that was right for them was that it was a big deal. People do not change homes every day. It's something you do rarely (sometimes only once!), and you might change every five or ten years or longer. In fact, according to the National Association of REALTORS®, in 2018, the median time people stayed in their homes was thirteen years.[2] So buying a home is a major decision and purchase, especially for those younger families or first-time buyers, and they're very appreciative. I'm still in touch with so many people whom we sold houses to. And I think part of it is that we didn't utilize a real estate agent, or that in-between person (something I discuss in the book). It all came directly to and from us, which made it kind of like keeping it in the family in our company.

I've also always wanted to combine my skill and desire to help people with business in one way or another. I've always been skilled at managing people and just managing in general—juggling all those balls in the air. I always knew I would do something in that direction. Then it so happened that when I moved to Texas, I settled in the greater Austin area. Without even knowing it, years ago, it was the perfect place to go into this kind of business because of growth in the area. Austin, between 2010 and 2020, experienced a population increase of 21 percent.[3] In competitive markets like Austin and elsewhere, people especially needed my service, which is why we established our headquarters in Austin.

With the success the house development brought us, API Inc. was able to grow and branch out into business acquisition. We now invest in other businesses, one of the main focuses being medical businesses; having a medical background makes the process easy and seamless. In short, house flipping opened up my world to so many opportunities, and I have learned so much along the way. Some people go into house flipping and continue with it forever, growing and scaling it. They may hold onto some properties as rentals or mix their portfolio. Others may use the experiences they gain from flipping to get into commercial real estate, development, or other areas.

As a successful house flipper and developer, I'm asked a lot of questions. Face it, we all have design questions, real estate questions. And because of all those home design and transformation shows, everyone is fascinated by house flipping. When I set out to write this book, I came up with the idea of a dictionary of sorts. Each letter represents a topic, a principle, or something you need to know before you consider entering into or investing in this field. Even if you have no interest in house flipping yourself but are considering buying a flipped home or investing in a company like mine or partnering with one, *The ABCs of Flipping: Your A-to-Z Guide to Buying, Rehabbing, and Selling Houses* will give you a solid background on the terms and ideas you need to know to educate yourself.

The knowledge and experience I have led me to want to show others how to do it—and what to do and not do. The pitfalls and pluses are all spelled out. If you aren't sure where to start, this guide is a gentle introduction.

So join me as we take a trip through the alphabet of house flipping. I hope to help you flip your life!

Analyzing the Market

Analyzing the market for your house-flipping business or investment is very important. This letter is not about choosing the house itself (we get into that more deeply in **C: Choose Wisely**). This is about the market as a whole. You must be educated on everything from supply chains to inventory to trends in the area you are working. If you are not, you could make costly mistakes—or be taken advantage of.

When I first started out as a house flipper, I spent a lot of time finding properties and being on the job sites themselves. This was my "baby." Later, as I put my team together (covered in **T: Teams**), a solid group of contractors, subcontractors, vendors, and others I had faith in, I could spend more time finding greater numbers of properties and analyzing market trends, some of the higher-level analyses my company needed.

Usually weekly, but at *least* twice a month, though, you want to check the following:

- Real estate association websites. While you want to know about individual REALTORS° in your area who are popular, selling a lot, specialists in a neighborhood you plan to work in, etc., real estate association websites will offer overall information for the area you are eyeing. They often have statistics for the market that will help you in your own personal analyses.

- Websites for the brokers. We will get into brokers in more detail in the letter *B*. These are more individual brokers—what they are selling, promoting, etc. Pay attention to how they market, to their brand, and to their specialties.

- Listings from wholesalers. Real estate wholesalers can be a very important part of your house-flipping business—and we will cover them in the letter *W*. For now, know they buy up many properties and attempt to sell off the contracts quickly, allowing house flippers to buy multiple properties from the wholesalers for a fee.

- Gross domestic product, inflation numbers, and supply chain issues. This is one of the great things about the internet and real estate. It's public; you can look at it. You can look at numbers, numbers, and more numbers. How are house prices trending? What is the inventory in your area? What parts of the supply chain are having difficulty? What are inflation or recession indicators?

When the prices are very high, demand is very high, and there are not enough houses for people looking to buy, you want to be flipping—renovating, reselling, and not holding onto houses or inventory because holding in a hot market does not make profitable sense.

In addition, for property owners, renting properties was less advisable during the height of the COVID-19 pandemic because there were restrictions, such as not evicting nonpaying tenants during the crisis. With the world uncertain, you now need to consider unusual market conditions.

When the market is "normal" (and let's face it, with so many changes in the world, we won't always know where or when that is for sure), when things are not quite so hot, you might consider a different approach, and buy, flip, and rent out properties (or do Airbnbs, which I discuss in **G: Geographic Locations**). You don't want to be *reactive*—waiting until the market totally shifts and then adapting to it. Instead, you want to be *proactive*, prepared for change before it happens.

Also be aware of the consumer price index, for example, and other market indicators. Unfortunately, television can

You want to be proactive, prepared for change before it happens.

give people an unrealistic idea of house flipping. For example, on TV, none of the "reality" flippers are shown analyzing the market, paying attention to the consumer price index, etc. Their flips are for a television program, streamlined for the cameras. No doubt, they analyze the same things I explore in the book—but you just don't see that.

ANALYZE THAT

What to look for in a house-flipping market analysis

1. Fast home sales. Are houses getting multiple offers on the same day it lists or you host an open house? How many days, on average, are homes on the market before they sell?

2. Are buyers trying to be competitive with cash-only deals or signing contracts without home inspections? Without contingencies?

3. Older homeowners? Older neighborhoods? Sometimes a whole neighborhood, in essence, is ripe for a flip. Older homeowners have raised their children and are looking to downsize or take off for Florida or the retirement city of their dreams.

4. Good schools. Good town. Good amenities. Low crime. We'll get into this in letter Z, but homeowners are looking for features in a town. Are houses walking distance from dining or shopping? Is there a neighborhood "feel"? Are the town's areas well kept and well lit? Is it located near main thoroughfares or highways leading to large employers in the area?

It's almost like the stock market (except, honestly, the returns on investing in house flipping can be much higher). You are analyzing not just the house itself, but the *market*, and you are watching for trends, just like in the stock market.

Brokers

The topic of brokers—should you become one, should you develop an exclusive relationship with one—is important for anyone entering house flipping or considering investing.

One of the more interesting things to consider is what the real estate market might look like in a decade. Will there even *be* real estate agents in ten years? As it is now, the version of real estate agent we usually think of might disappear because there are so many newer services, such as Zillow, Opendoor, and—I am sure as I am writing this—new, emerging apps. According to the US Bureau of Labor Statistics, real estate brokers are expected to have very low growth (about 4 percent) as a profession over the next decade.[4] An Oxford study determined real estate is an area where computerization/tech is going to make sharp inroads.[5]

Apps like DocuSign and others mean the real estate business is more around the clock than ever (like much of life). Transactions can move fast—and some things can be done on a smartphone. Sites like Redfin and for-sale-by-owner kits are making sellers reconsider their use of REALTORS˙.

There are also new sales methods. We've all seen the ads on TV for companies that buy damaged, run-down, and unattractive houses. Though the offer will be below market value, it is nonetheless a different approach to acquiring houses. Virtual tours, social media networking, even lotteries … real estate sales just don't look like they used to.

In addition, today's buyer is a *lot* savvier. They can look up any question online (which can be a good thing or a bad thing, as not all information out there is accurate). They also tend to come to an agent with an already-clear idea of what they want—they've looked at hundreds of homes online. They may even come to a real estate agent having already picked out the house and just wanting the agent to walk them through the process.

So if you are a house flipper, should you also be a broker?

I personally chose not to have my broker's license. But before I made that decision, I analyzed the ins and outs of studying and obtaining a real estate license for a house-flipping business. Here are some important considerations:

- Getting your license will give you very good insights into property law in the state where you are trying to flip houses. Every state is different.

- You will have access to the Multiple Listing Services available to real estate agents, commonly known as the MLS. It is important to note that if you have a good relationship with a broker, in essence that also gains you access.

- You can list your own properties on the MLS. You'll also have your finger on the pulse of what's new on there as listings are added.

- As a broker, you gain extra income, especially when starting out in house flipping. You can make sales on the side and meld the two income streams.

- Many house flippers are brokers because they can get that "first look" at properties.

- Clients may feel more comfortable if you have your real estate broker's license.

- You save a commission fee.

- You save on closing costs. (In most places, you need to have a real estate agent present at closing/handling it.)

Two drawbacks are:

- Time. I was so busy when I first started my business that I did not have time to pursue my license—and I had forged some good relationships with agents. Depending on your state, you can plan on spending four to six months on the course itself, and then there will be hours you spend studying and training.

- Money. It costs money to earn your real estate license. You have courses, fees for licensing itself, fees for memberships, and costs associated with your own background check. If you are just starting in the flipping business, cost will probably be one of your concerns.

In addition, think of the reasons you are considering going into house flipping. Chances are your answers might include making money (obviously), creativity, the excitement of finding and transforming homes, etc. You most likely are not thinking, "Oh, it will be so exciting and so much fun to learn all the boring fine print of real estate contracts and regulations!" Much of the "people" aspect and fun aspect of real estate is *not* part of getting your license—it is very much about the nitty-gritty legal and fine print, statutes, laws—the boring stuff (that you *must* be aware of—or have a broker you trust). Consider your personality and whether that is something that you would like to be involved in as you form your business.

If you decide to work with a broker instead of becoming one yourself, here are some suggestions for choosing one, based on Zillow's checklist:

Check out the local housing market in person. Before you sign with a broker, you should pay a visit to the market you are working in (especially if it is not your home base; we will discuss long-distance flipping in **G: Geographic Location**). You want a broker who has connections to the community, has networks and contacts, who seems to really *know* their chosen market intimately. You need to have a feel for that market as well. There are some things you just can't fully sense about a place until you walk the neighborhood or drive through at different times of the day or evening. Does downtown become a ghost town after five? How bad is traffic at rush hour? It's important to know a market intimately—and if you can't, because you are very busy with your business, you want a broker who does know it.

- Take meetings with three to four agents. See their selling/communication style—does it mesh with yours? Do they follow up and call/show up when they say they are going to? How do they handle showings, etc.? Talk to them about the details that are important to you and your business.

Clarify your motivations to sell. Make sure the broker you choose has experience dealing with house flippers and understands that selling quickly is essential. House flippers are different kinds of buyers, as well. You want a broker who has worked with investors not just individuals looking to buy their dream home. I've had brokers show me "perfect" homes in need of little renovation—that didn't fit my business model.

- Check referrals. If you don't have your broker's license, you are trusting this person to watch out for your interests. Ask for—and speak to—referrals.

- Do they use nontraditional selling strategies? How are they leveraging social media? What is their marketing like?[6]

You have different needs from a young couple wanting to tour ten houses to find their dream home to start a family. So you need a broker who understands this. Most real estate agents are wired for just your average seller or buyer who are selling/buying a house for themselves or are looking for a house as a family. As a house flipper, you want to

As a house flipper, you want to seek out a real estate agent who is investor friendly.

seek out a real estate agent who is investor friendly. They are not all like that.

Investor-friendly real estate agents are the type I actually used at the beginning when we just started. They will be very prepared in the area of market analysis because they are used to working with investors. You are trying to maximize your profits—not find your ideal home. In fact, you are most likely looking for distressed homes and fixer-uppers.

These investor-friendly real estate brokers are also more likely to have off-market listings, allowing you to snap up properties before they become available to others.

Look for REI certification. Real Estate Investing (REI) is a certification offered by the National Association of REALTORS®. They define it as follows: "The Real Estate Investing certification program is for REALTORS® who want to master the ins and outs of working with investors and those who are establishing themselves as real estate investors."[7]

I also worked with flat-fee real estate agencies. Both REI-certified and flat-fee real estate agents are used to working with investors ready to move fast. The REI-certified agent has had specialized training on the needs of investors. They charge a percentage fee (as most real estate agents typically do). A flat-fee agent charges a fee—not a percentage. The fee is usually a few thousand dollars, depending on the market. This generally saves you money—and when moving a lot of inventory, it can pay off in the long run.

They can show you a few houses a day, help you make offers very fast, etc. It's a little bit different pace, a little bit different market—they are not taking you to five or six houses that meet your "dream" criteria, as if you were going to buy and live in the home yourself. In other words, you're not letting them know "I need three bedrooms, two bathrooms, a home office, and I really want a wood-burning fireplace, stainless appliances, and a separate dining room for when my partner and I entertain." Instead, they are taking you, rather quickly, through many potential investor homes, usually undervalued houses needing work in desirable neighborhoods.

I know there are some great agents out there. If you are new to the industry, having a reliable, knowledgeable agent can help you once you bid, with the paperwork, and so on. But just make sure your agent knows your needs. Homes that are too expensive leave no margin for profit. Investor-friendly real estate agents are frequently more seasoned in this aspect of the business.

Choose Wisely

Analyzing the market, which we covered in letter *A*, is about the big picture. Is this the time—and is this the place/market—to be in the house-flipping business? And what do you need to consider as far as inventory, selling, and renting?

But now we're going to look at what is important when choosing an actual house to flip.

The Cost

Obviously, the first thing that I mentally calculated whenever I drove up to a property or looked at it online was the cost. Trust me, after the first six or seven houses you flip, you have a calculator in your head. The calculator has two settings: *What am I going to do/have to do?* (to the house) and *How much is it going to cost?*

Certain things can't be fixed with a coat of paint.

Will the house you are considering be profitable? (See the 70 Percent Rule on the next page; also, in **H: Home Inspection,** there is a checklist in table 1, that lists all the things I try to roughly calculate and examine when I walk into a potential home.)

You need to figure out what you are going to have to put into the house—and will it still be profitable? You also must know what the current market demands as far as extras, rooms, and so on. For instance, there have been quite a few houses where we added rooms or closed off an area for an office. Even if it's a very average-sized house, you can create an office for the buyers—add a wall here and there. Especially with the changes to the workforce that have occurred because of the COVID-19 pandemic, many, if not most, people are looking for space to have their Zoom calls, to work from the house, at least part time or in a hybrid situation.

As of this writing, generally people still like having an open floor plan. In another era, houses had many small rooms—so this is something you frequently see in older homes. Removing a couple of walls changes a home's energy and flow. I also am a big believer in putting in bigger windows that allow more light. But, of course, these things cost money. However, as we'll discuss in the next section on the potential, there are certain upgrades that will nearly always reap rewards in terms of sale price.

THE 70 PERCENT RULE

Most home flippers use the 70 Percent Rule to determine whether to purchase a home. This is the estimated value of the house after repairs are made as well as the estimated repair costs using this simple formula:

After-repair value (ARV) × 0.70 – Estimated repair costs = Maximum buying price

The Potential

As a house flipper, you have to learn to see past the ugly and the old and envision the potential of a house. Ignore the orange shag carpet, the hideous wallpaper, the dated vanity in the bathroom, and the atrocious green paint job on the outside.

As I already mentioned, just allowing in more light in an older home can make a big difference. Cosmetic changes accomplish so much. Here are some of the most common upgrades you should consider for your flip as you analyze the potential of a home:

Just allowing in more light in an older home can make a big difference. Cosmetic changes accomplish so much.

- What sort of shape is the kitchen in? What are some of the obvious flip fixes you can make? Paint? Tile? A backsplash? New floors? Stainless appliances? Pendant lights? In older homes, you will see that kitchens used to be their own rooms, set off from the living room or dining room. These days, families gravitate toward open spaces, where conversation can flow or parents can prepare meals while also interacting with their kids or overseeing homework. Islands are something most homeowners look for these days. We will get into design later, but keep in mind that you are making changes for the average home buyer, regardless of your personal taste. Putting a single slab of expensive marble imported from Italy is not likely to be recouped in a $225,000 starter home.

- Updating bathrooms with a crisp new look. A bathroom can go from *blah* to *wow* with great lighting, fresh paint, a new vanity, and accessories. You don't always have to gut a bathroom or reconfigure the flooring or layout. Learn to see past dated tile and dim lighting.

- Landscaping and curb appeal. I know someone who almost bought a too-small town house for herself and her husband and new baby because of the patio garden. It was stunning, with a small koi pond, brilliant-hued flowers, and paving stones and outdoor furniture that completed the oasis feel. The outside almost "sold her." A pop of color on a front door, new shrubbery and flowers, fresh mulch; all of it can be done without spending a fortune. Don't forget curb appeal when completing your flip, because more and more people view outdoor entertainment spaces as part of their lifestyle and home.

- Floors. Clients and I were often amazed when we pulled up old carpeting in a 1980s rust-colored shag—only to discover perfect wood floors beneath. We were not often that lucky, alas. However, new flooring is often an imperative. No one wants to move into a house with stained carpeting or scuffed wood floors. Again, learn to see past the ugly to the potential.

- Windows and lights. As I mentioned, replacing windows is often a wise decision. Bringing light into a dim home makes all the difference. In addition, when staging a house to sell it, use lighting to brighten and focus your rooms.

- The roof. If you have good relationships with contractors and subcontractors, meaning you get good, fair pricing because you are giving them consistent work, a new roof should not be a dealbreaker. Unless a roof is newer, I generally always replaced it so that there was no chance of leaks and other water damage.

When to Pause or Walk Away

I want to be honest—one of the reasons I wrote this book is to help others not make some of the same mistakes I made when starting out. I will never forget a painful lesson I learned when I toured a home that was certainly going to be snatched up. Austin real estate was so competitive, and there was little inventory. I toured the home, and I saw so much potential. I knew I could flip it fast. But there was a catch. Because the market was so intense, buyers were offering to purchase the house with no inspection.

I am sure you know where this story is going. Against my better judgment, I bought the house on sight, perhaps swept up in my enthusiasm. Once we got working on it, though, I discovered the house had major foundation issues. This required literally lifting the house and extensive work. I turned a profit—but it was far less, obviously, than had I not run into this problem.

Here's a list of some issues that should make you walk away—or at least hit a strong pause:

- Major foundational issues. This should be a straight cost calculator. Foundational issues are one of those things that are not going to be fixed with a coat of paint. You need to calculate the cost of fixing versus the potential sales price (use the 70 Percent Rule). Certainly, in lower-priced homes, it is unlikely you would recoup the costs to the level you need to consider the flip worth it.

- A neighborhood with issues of crime or upkeep. People want to know their children can go out for a bike ride in their own neighborhood and feel safe. Neighborhoods with high crime or multiple houses that are clearly in need of extensive repairs can be a sign not to purchase. You can fix a house. You cannot fix its neighborhood. Another red flag would be a house very near to an industrial area, a highway with a lot of noise, an airport, etc. I recall a funny episode of a house-selling show. A gentleman in Chicago fell in love with a woman with small children. When they married, he wanted to sell his bachelor pad, and they were moving into a larger town house in the city that could accommodate this new little family. The problem was his condo backed *directly* up to train tracks. He thought the sounds of the train were evocative or romantic. Unfortunately, few buyers shared his vision. He couldn't up and move the condo. Some things cannot be overcome. (Though he did apparently find a train-loving buyer.)

- Very old houses. As I said, I would not walk away from a solid house in need of a new roof (depending on the circumstances, obviously); however, very old homes often have hidden problems. A seasoned house flipper will likely know what to look for (though even then, there are surprises), but I especially would not recommend this for a new home flipper. There could be lead paint, asbestos, radon gas, mold in the walls, outdated plumbing and wiring, etc. In addition, if it happens to be historic, there may be ordinances and rules regarding your updating or changing its facade, etc.

- Sprinkler system and fencing issues. Believe it or not, on a large property, sprinkler system issues (with their leaks beneath the surface) can be an expensive proposition to fix. The same with fencing, depending on the size of the property. Many people want a fenced yard. Fifty-six percent of the US population owns at least one dog.[8] People with children want a place they know their kids are safe to play. A decent fence (and I do not like to cut corners and put up just anything) are costly. Replacing a badly damaged one will cost you—so use the 70 Percent Rule as you add it all up.

- Air conditioning systems; plumbing. These are two house systems that can cause a large number of headaches in a house flip or remodel if there are significant issues. Plumbing issues can be hidden behind walls. Wiring issues too. You want a good **H: Home Inspection** to ensure you don't find surprises.

- Environmental contamination/mold. If a home inspection reveals toxic mold or other environmental issues, this is usually a sign that the home could be a very large problem you do not want to take on. House flipping requires a fast turnover—and these are often things that cannot be fixed quickly.

Decorating and Design

For most fans of house-flipping television shows, the decorating and design portion is the most fun part to watch. It is amazing how design flourishes, paint, lighting, new windows, new cabinets, etc. can make a house unrecognizable from its former life. Some flippers have real vision—they are able to see how removing a wall here or adding a breakfast bar here or built-in there can change a room and update a house. So let's look at the ins and outs of decorating and design for your house-flipping project.

Do Your Research

Most design shows depict a designer going into a home, waving their arms, and saying, "We'll do this and that," and voilà! A new home! They will often create a three-dimensional computer model, and then let's not forget they have relationships with places with the nicest, trendiest furnishings, home goods, and finishes. (Not to mention a large team to make all of it come true—often with custom carpenters and other craftspeople.) However, the process is actually not just gut instinct and big ideas. It takes research and thought.

First, at least once a year, do research on what's trending now—including in the area you are working in (see the next section: "Regional Decor"). If you've ever looked at a listing online of an older home with overwhelming floral or chintz wallpaper or rag-roll painting from the 1980s, gold fixtures from the 1990s, or block-glass bathroom windows from another era, you know that styles come in and go out—and when they go out, it makes a home very dated. Additionally, some choices of yesteryear, such as pink-tiled and pink-tubbed bathrooms, were especially unwise choices, as it committed the homeowner to a color choice that could not be overcome with a can of paint. (And which will have to be replaced in your flip!)

Therefore, while there are trends, you should also aim to be as *timeless* as possible. If you follow a trend, choose the more universally appealing looks without going too edgy.

What are home buyers looking for right now?

- Lighter colors—gray is very in right now, but beiges, soft whites, and crisp, clean, light paint choices are also the way to go. I always painted my homes in shades of cream. Go neutral all the way. Then, when staging your flip, you can use pops of color in throw pillows, rugs, or accents, without committing to it in a paint color or tiles. This will (in my opinion) be a style that stays regardless of the times. When jewel-toned walls were in, it basically committed people to a very heavy color palette. If that is not your style, it could be overwhelming.

Neutrals can *always* have accents of what's trendy. In addition, neutrals can be painted over without needing coats of primer.

- Open floor plans—home buyers want good flow. When people are cooking or entertaining, they want to be able to interact with their kids or guests instead of being shut off in a different room. If you stage your home, beware of furniture that blocks flow and natural pathways from room to room. (Some people even turn to the ancient art of feng shui to ensure a home has good energy.)

- Big windows. I cannot imagine a time when natural light will no longer be in. Light lifts the mood and makes everything cleaner and brighter. In cities, condos, or apartments, there is often a concern for how much (if any) natural light an apartment gets. In houses, overgrown bushes and trees that block natural light should be trimmed back. When my company does a flip, we do not put in window treatments. First, window treatments are so varied—you are spending money and *time* (important for a flip) creating window treatments the homeowner will likely redo or will not be to their taste. If it's too standard or inexpensive (such as plain shades or blinds) the new owners are *definitely* going to take them out. And without window treatments, more light comes in for showing.

- Tall ceilings open up a room. Obviously, if you buy a home to flip, the ceilings are part of the structure of the flip. But where possible, you can add crown molding or other design elements that draw the eye upward.

- Patio, deck, or designated outdoor entertaining space. Depending on what area of the country you are flipping in, outdoor space can mean a year-round extra entertainment area. (Personally, I am not a fan of Texas's hot summers—but plenty of my friends and neighbors eat and entertain outside year round!) Rather than simply showing an open yard, creating a seating/entertaining area adds a completeness to the space. Don't forget landscaping, stones, or other features to spruce up a backyard space.

- Walk-in closets, especially in the master. If you cannot fully transform a closet, use mirrors and lighting inside the closet to open up the look of it and make it feel more spacious.

- Walk-in pantries. Many older homes do not have pantries, and it's something today's homeowners feel they can't live without. (I know I couldn't.) We always did whatever we could to create such a space if one didn't exist.

- "Hardwood" flooring. I put that in quotation marks. Beautiful hardwood floors, freshly resanded and stained, are an ideal. But increasingly, the look is being achieved with premium, high-end laminates, luxury vinyl tiling (LVTs, very popular at the moment), and other flooring types that give the same/similar look with the benefits of being waterproof and more pet and child resistant.

- Carpet in the bedrooms. If you choose to keep hardwood in the bedrooms, consider staging with a rug. People tend to desire a warmer bedroom feel that carpeting offers.

- Updated kitchen with stainless appliances. Kitchen remodels recoup their investment more than any other home remodel element. Again, look at what's trending. For example, though it might sound like a small detail, it used to be that cabinets in the kitchen stopped a little bit below the ceiling—people used to put artificial plants, decorating items, or display items, etc. up there. Now cabinets go all the way to the ceiling (a bit more expensive for the house flipper, but again, what the market demands).

- An island in the kitchen—I made this its own bullet point. Today's kitchens almost always demand this. Again, the way we view our kitchens is no longer shut off from the rest of the family, but instead it is where the family *gathers*. Islands with bar stool seating, breakfast bars, etc. are items today's homeowner wants. When people entertain, their friends can gather there while one person cooks. It affords more expansive space for preparing food. It's simply something today's home buyer wants.

- Natural stone, granite, or quartz countertops. Today's buyers are looking for natural woods, natural stone, and that very zen, neutral, serene feeling.

- Spacious bathrooms. Very often a tub is something clients want—for young families, it allows them to bathe toddlers. For adults, they envision soaking in the bath (even though, let's be honest, we all *think* we are going to do that and never do—it's a highly underused feature for many). Oftentimes we don't put a bathtub in when there is not that much space in houses we flip. Instead, we create a shower with a fabulous rainfall showerhead and gorgeous new tiling.

- There's an adage in the real estate business: "Kitchens and bathrooms sell the house." Heed that!

- Don't be afraid to paint brick. I often did this on both fire-places and exteriors (in fact, if a house is not selling, consider repainting the exterior—it often does the trick). A fireplace can be a great focal point in a living room or den, as many people list a fireplace as a want. Don't forget a show-stopping mantel.

- Use mirrors, lights, or chandeliers with twinkling crystals (always popular), LED lights, etc. to add even more light into your space.

REGIONAL DECOR

I live in Texas—where Texas style is everything. As you drive through Austin, you'll see the Lone Star affixed on the front of houses or hanging above a garage near the roofline. Wooden Americana-style decor is common. Barn door–style interior doors are in. Home buyers in Texas want that rustic look and feel.

Depending on where you are flipping a house, you must keep in mind what is hot in your market.

Depending on where you are flipping a house, you must keep in mind what is hot in your market. A home just outside Manhattan is not likely to want the Lone Star look. A home in a ski resort town is not right for coastal style.

To give some examples, here are some regional differences according to Living Spaces:[9]

- Boho style is popular in Maryland, Illinois, Ohio, North Carolina, and elsewhere. It's breezy and comfortable, with that funky hint of eclecticism. Light, with the use of natural materials.

- The clean lines of contemporary are more popular in New York, Arizona, New Jersey, and Florida. This is a very classic look. The sleek lines of a New York apartment or a Florida condominium are the right fit for contemporary. New York City apartments often choose sleek contemporary so as not to distract from the big selling attraction—a skyline view.

- Coastal style is popular in Delaware, as well as beachfront properties nearly everywhere. This uses neutrals, soft blues, and natural woods. There may be nautical touches.

- Farmhouse style is trending in Connecticut and Tennessee. This is an eclectic, welcoming look.

- Industrial style is hot in Maine, Oregon, and here in Texas. This works with materials like metal and wood. Lines are clean and modern with an edge.

- Midcentury modern is popular in Washington, DC, California, North Dakota, and Alaska.

- The simplicity and beauty of Scandinavian design are a plus in Hawaii and Idaho.

This may change. Fads and trends come and go. That's why it's imperative you keep up on what is popular where you are flipping. At the same time, keep budget in mind! Look for ways to use design trends without spending a fortune.

⌂ FLIP TIP

IT'S NOT YOUR HOUSE

It can be tempting—especially if you are a fan of design and decor or if you have a creative streak—to decorate a house to your taste. There is a temptation to choose finishes you love or a set of pendant lights straight out of Dale Chihuly style—even if they cost a bit more—because they represent your aesthetic. After all, you want to be very proud of the house you are flipping—you want it to be memorable, to have people ooh and aah at the open house. But while you do not want to put in cheap finishes or cut corners to where the house suffers, keep in mind this is not your house. Also keep in mind the price point. Do not lose sight of the 70 Percent Rule. A modest house in a modest neighborhood may not recoup marble and travertine and a new spa shower with inlaid mosaic tile and twenty spa jets.

DON'T FORGET THE LITTLE THINGS

House flipping also requires that you don't forget the little things. You are looking at the big picture—the big ways you can improve a home. But sometimes those little things are details a buyer will notice.

Here's a simple example. Choose finishes (door pulls, cabinet pulls, etc.) that are fresh and new and don't look cheap. Don't reface cabinets and simply put the old hardware on. Fresh light switches. Fresh outlet covers. These are not things that add an obvious dollar value to a home. But they are things that look tacky or undone if not handled properly.

Silly thing, and it also might not be something you notice, but when I was flipping houses, we never installed the toilet paper roll holder in the bathroom. Why? Because we wanted the look of a clean, freshly painted, uninterrupted wall when showing the house.

Don't forget lights—and that *includes* in your outdoor space. Something as simple as stringing modern outdoor LED lights with a trattoria feel or a sleek industrial look can transform a space in a yard, along with staging a few nice pieces of outdoor furniture. Lights can work to create a boundary or box in an area as an outside room without spending for a she shed.

In bathrooms, use bright lighting around the vanity or mirror. You could redo a bathroom beautifully—but it won't do you any good if the bathroom is dark!

Another small detail to not overlook is the scent of a home. When a potential buyer walks in, the house should smell "new," fresh, and also not overly perfumed. A few reed diffusers scattered throughout the house, scents like linen, which tend not to be too floral and overwhelming, are simple tips to apply in your home flip.

FLIP TIP

FIND YOUR FINISHES

If you find finishes, light fixtures, etc. that work across different styles of home and that look clean and sleek, buy them in bulk to use on all or most of your flip projects so you don't have to waste time deciding what finishes to put in each house.

In addition, with supply chain issues, buying in bulk ensures you have the finishes you want—and don't run out or have them on back order or, worse, unavailable halfway through the process. And keep in mind—your finishes should match throughout the house. Don't have brass in the kitchen and silver in the guest bathroom.

LUXURY FLIPS

Flips of high-end houses tend to be less common. The main reason is that it is more difficult to find a true luxury home that is undervalued and thus ripe for a flip. Everything about these flips, if you take one on, is more expensive.

Here's a simple example. A few years ago, a snap of vicious cold weather hit parts of Texas. Because of the unexpected shock of freezing weather, countless majestic palm trees died. Replacing them with mature palms—along with the landscaping and installation costs, etc.—can run into the thousands and thousands of dollars for a few trees lining a driveway.

These are the sorts of homes where, for example, it is advisable to install an outside fireplace or kitchen and other high-end perks—and the appliances and other finishes are more costly. You also need to be sure to have a wow factor—a grand foyer or some element that takes people's breath away and makes your home memorable.

Generally, you will need the following in a luxury flip: real hardwood floors, natural stone, elaborate or high-end backsplashes in the kitchen, luxury showers with stone and multijets, custom kitchen cabinets—luxury flips have customers who appreciate the different kinds of wood. Luxury home buyers are more likely to be concerned about tech—smart homes, green and sustainable features. They may also want a media room, a yoga room, and a charging station for an electric car. But you shouldn't guess. When investing in a luxury flip, learn as much as you can about the neighborhood and some of the standard upgrades that most of them have.

(🏠) **FLIP TIP**

KEEP IT SIMPLE

I once chose a wow-factor chandelier for a house. The piece was beautiful. I only discovered when it shipped to us that there were over a hundred pieces to assemble. You are always against the clock in a flip. I think we stayed up until three in the morning putting this together. The lesson? Keep it *simple*. Find beautiful pieces that look fabulous—but are assembled easily and quickly.

POOLS AND SPAS

Perhaps you picture a beautiful pool with crystal-clear water in the backyard of your house flip, surrounded by gently swaying palms. I am here to tell you that swimming pools generally do not bring any value to the house. Many people are leery of the responsibility (especially those with small children because of the risk of accidental drowning). Pools always bring more maintenance. If you are buying a flip in poorer condition, you can be sure there are going to be issues with an uncared-for pool. Sometimes, it is simpler to fill it in than make all the necessary repairs (or redo the pool in its entirety).

In a luxury flip, depending on the area, you might need a pool or hot tub. For example, in a place like Florida, home pools are common. If a luxury flip has a poorly maintained pool (perhaps if the home went into foreclosure), it will likely be worth it to redo it completely, put that beautiful tile on its edges, and make it look inviting. You can even add a hot tub or spa.

Staging the Scene

I would say we staged approximately 80 percent of our houses, and 20 percent we didn't stage because we got offers before we even put them on the market. However, as of this writing, the market is hot, with some indicators it may cool.

In general, though, you want to stage your houses. This allows people to envision how the rooms can be used, where a couch will fit, or where the new homeowner would position the bed in a master suite. Unless you have a warehouse full of extra furniture that looks brand new (which you would have to pay storage on) and depending on how many homes you are trying to sell at a time, it makes sense to hire a staging firm and pay a monthly fee for their furniture and accents instead of doing it yourself.

Staging also lets you show off rooms the way you're trying to propose them. For example, suppose there is an empty room right next to the entrance. Not every home buyer has the vision to know how to utilize their space. But it could be a great office or playroom or a perfect spot for a reading nook. By staging it, the room is no longer a question mark but a place the potential buyer can see for their home.

Kitchens and bathrooms sell a house!

It is especially important to stage the living room, kitchen, master bedroom, and all the bathrooms (bathrooms are a very simple stage, as no furniture is involved). It is OK to leave spare bedrooms empty (or just stage one as a guestroom). Remember the adage: Kitchens and bathrooms sell a house!

We will discuss your team in the letter *T*, but you will want to establish a relationship with your stager. When I was just starting, many of the best stagers were booked. No one knew me or my work yet. Meanwhile, their existing clients of course had priority. Over time, through networking and contacts, I established my own relationships with stagers I like.

One other consideration regarding staging is cost. In a hot market where homes are selling in weeks (and in some places, in days), cost is not a huge consideration, as prices are driving upward. As markets cool or return to normal, a house might sit on the market for six months—when paying a monthly staging fee, that can add up, particularly over multiple homes. Some flippers may save money by only staging the first floor in a two-story house, for example.

The little things count when staging too. Pops of color, on-trend looks, fresh flowers on the table, fresh scents, lighting all set; nothing too personal—but not totally stark and cold either.

Entity and Image

Some people, especially those new to flipping, may flip under their own name, house by house. Perhaps they are making sure they like this new profession or side hustle. Perhaps it's a cost factor—having to set up a corporation, hire an attorney, hire an accountant, etc. However, it is my belief that entity and image are essential to being a successful real estate flipper or investor.

Taxes, Incorporating, the Law, and You

I am not an accountant or a lawyer, so my advice is based on my own experiences. However, before you even *think* about actually doing a house flip, I would suggest consulting with a lawyer and an accountant. Every state has different laws, regulations, tax issues, etc. related to real estate and flipping. Here are just a couple of examples of issues that pertain to real estate investing on the legal or tax side:

- If you are buying and selling houses individually under your own name, you are going to have tax implications. "The standard tax consequences of flipping a house, where you own the property for less than twelve months, is that the profit you make is subject to your standard taxation rate. This is due to the fact that the IRS classes any investment you own for less than a year then sell for a profit as 'normal income.'"[10]

- Some states have laws on the books requiring house flippers to have a contracting license.

- Depending on your financing, there could be red flags to lenders that you are engaging in mortgage fraud, even if you are not.[11]

- Distressed properties sometimes have title issues (for example, if a home is in foreclosure or there are multiple liens on it).

In short, this isn't the type of entrepreneurial adventure in which to wing it. I understand if this is initially a side job or supplemental income, there is a desire to start slowly. But consider that if things take off and you have to retroactively resolve issues, it will cost you more money in the long run. Additionally, if things take off, guess what? You will have less time than ever to deal with all this. Better to establish your entity and identity from the beginning.

There are a number of ways to establish your entity, from a limited liability corporation (LLC) to a corporation (either an S-corporation or a C-corporation). Tax implications are different for each. Which should you choose? *That's* why you talk to an accountant and a lawyer.

What's in a Name?

Once you decide on the entity of your company, you need to establish your identity. There is a slogan in Austin: "Keep Austin weird." (Venice in California has the same slogan— "Keep Venice weird.") I applaud that— but when it comes to your company name, *weird* is probably not the way to go.

> **People are entrusting you with probably the *biggest* purchase they will make in their lives.**

People are entrusting you with probably the *biggest* purchase they will make in their lives. Sounding eccentric or having a name that is confusing or so unusual that few people know what it means (or how to pronounce it) is not reassuring. You likely want something that sounds more classic and established.

Here are some things to consider as you pick a company name:

- Don't pick a name too close to your competitors or a nationally known real estate company. You don't want people confusing the two of you.

- Make sure people know how to pronounce your company's name. Not only is this important because people do not like feeling foolish and not knowing how to pronounce something; this is even *more important* today as people use Siri and voice-activated searches. (I cannot be the only one who has been frustrated with Siri as she mishears a word I think I am pronouncing clearly!)

- Make sure the name is easy to spell, without confusing things. For example, avoid things like "Homes for You Too"—if someone heard that, is it "too" or "two"? In short, if you have to *spell out* the name of your company for someone, your company name is already a problem.

- Make sure your company name is web friendly—no hyphens, back slashes, underscores, or any punctuation. Also make sure your web address is not very different from the actual name (i.e., doesn't use abbreviations, shortened names, etc.—some people do this when they cannot get the domain name of their choice).

Do Your Homework

Once you select the name, I would suggest going to your state's Secretary of State website to make sure there is no other company with that name and then buy the domain for it.

I will be honest in that there are plenty of companies out there that charge money to teach people about house flipping. Some will say, "Just go out there and do it! Flip your first house!" I suppose it is a difference in philosophy. I want to do things the right way from the very beginning. If I am going to do something, I am going to give it 100 percent; I am going to learn everything I possibly can about it.

To me, if you are retroactively trying to create a business entity or you do not have these things established properly, you are saying to me that you are not taking this as seriously as you should or could be. Dream big!

There are also fewer businesswomen compared to businessmen, let alone women CEOs. As a woman in a highly competitive field, I want the edge of a strong corporate identity.

What Is Your Brand?

A brand is more than a company name. According to Investopedia,[12] the term brand refers to a business and marketing concept that helps people identify a particular company, product, or individual. Brands are intangible, which means you can't actually touch or see them. As such, they help shape people's perceptions of companies, their products, or individuals. Brands commonly use identifying markers to help create brand identities within the marketplace. They provide enormous value to the company or individual, giving them a competitive edge over others in the same industry. As such, many entities seek legal protection for their brands by obtaining trademarks.

Have you thought about what sort of brand you want for your house-flipping company or real estate investment company? What do you want your company to be known for? Here are some examples of brand identities and ideas for house-flipping companies:

- Are you known for rehabbing certain neighborhoods? Are you part of that community?

- Are your kitchens, floors, built-ins, or some other aspect of your flips distinctive? If you think of some of the branded house flips on television shows, certain designers/flippers have a signature look—whether that's a farmhouse look or giving all their houses a Craftsman feel or certain signature flourishes in the kitchen. What is your wow factor on all your houses?

- Be genuine. Remember when I mentioned that many of my former clients call me months and years later to tell me how much they are still so thrilled with their house? That is because I always genuinely cared about providing houses that families would love and live in for years. We all know the difference between a salesperson we might label "slick" and one who actually sits down and gets to know the client. Be known for caring and people will return to you for their next house, and the next and the next (and they'll recommend you to their friends).

- Is your logo, website, etc. professional or does it look like a fifth-grade classroom project? What does your online presence say about you? What is your social media footprint?

- Are the staging and photographs of the home professional? In this era of Instagram, the bar is set pretty high. Make sure the lighting is great. Do dramatic before-and-afters. Consider hiring a professional photographer (and drone filmographer).

Financing

Financing is a vast topic and as varied as house flippers and their lenders. Your accountant and lawyer can handle much of this—but you should be aware of all your options. I'm going to go over some of the broad categories of financing for your house-flipping business.

All Cash

If only we all had $200,000 in cash hidden under our mattress. Of course, I am kidding, but all-cash offers are not as rare as they used to be.

For example, Austin is a very hot market at the moment. During the height of the COVID-19 pandemic, over $634 million was spent by foreign investors buying Austin properties.[13] Austin is also a landlord-friendly market, which also makes it attractive to those wanting to hop into the real estate market. According to Austin's NPR station, one-third of houses bought since 2020 were purchased by investors.[14]

In short, a very hot market like that is a terrible market for regular people to go and buy houses (hate to be the bearer of bad news). If you are a young family trying to buy your first home, you're up against bidders who have cash. Often lots of it. Even a qualifying mortgage letter is not as effective a bidding element as cash. For house flippers, the same is true. If you are buying distressed homes, where you must make decisions quickly, in a tight market you are going to go up against people and companies with a lot more money and experience than you, many who have cash in hand.

Is cash a possibility? What if you partnered with someone (discussed later in this chapter)?

Hard Money Lenders

If you have only ever applied for and obtained a traditional mortgage for a family home, you may not be familiar with the term *hard money lenders*. These loans are for the short term—because you are getting a higher-interest loan that you will want to pay off quickly. The application process and the approval process are streamlined and faster—something attractive for flippers who are trying to turn over properties as quickly as possible. You will usually offer 10 to 20 percent as a down payment. In addition, in most cases you will get the loan more easily than with a traditional bank or government loan because the credit restrictions are less stringent. Because of this, your lender is taking a higher risk on you. They will actually be private investors, not a bank. And because of that risk factor, they will charge you higher interest.

Because these kinds of loans are designed for the flipping or investing industry, sometimes these are nicknamed "fix-flip loans." The name says it all.

Hard money lenders can be individuals, private investors, or national companies (but not banks). As private investors, hard money lenders can set interest rates and credit score requirements and debt-to-income ratios on their own, without regard to prevailing market rates and standards. The collateral (aside from your down payment) is the property you are buying. Should something go seriously wrong with your flip or you are somehow left holding the house, these loans have a short repayment period—years, not decades. Therefore, that's the risk to *you*.

What kind of interest rates are we talking about? Let's say the prevailing interest rate is 3.5 percent. A hard money lender might offer an interest rate of 8 percent—or higher.

Once you are established with a hard money lender who has seen you do a few successful flips, it is even easier for you to work with them. But when you are new, this can be difficult. They don't know if you can handle all the ins and outs of flipping your investment property. You are untested.

This then may lead to another creative way of financing your flip—finding investment partners.

Partnering

Sometimes you may have the knowledge and passion (and background as a contractor, say) to flip houses—but not the money. This can be an opportunity to partner with someone. You bring the muscle, work, supervision, creative ideas, find the property, etc., and your investor provides the capital to get you going. Sometimes a partner might be another flipper—but you each excel in different areas. Maybe you have a contractor's license and are an experienced remodeler, and they have relationships with wholesalers and have some connections to private investors and so can handle the financing side.

Since house flipping has been made so popular by TV shows and magazines, I've even heard of groups of friends going into business together, where they each put in money, do the work together, and split the profits. Obviously, if you do this with six friends, you're not each going to make a fortune—but if this is the business for you, it's a start! It will give you experience and get a couple of flips under your belt until you feel ready to do one on your own.

Conventional Loans

Conventional loans for a house flip are a little more difficult in that they have more hoops to jump through and they work a bit slower. Nonetheless, if you are starting out as a house flipper, you may be able to get a conventional loan if the following applies to you:[15]

- You already have assets for collateral. This can be your own primary home, a vacation home, as well as stocks, etc. (Beware: collateral means you are putting those items at risk.)

- You are not doing a fast flip. There are some people who will buy a flip, live in it as a primary residence, fix it up, and sell and move on. This isn't a pathway to make a lot of money, as you are doing one at a time, but it does allow you to do a regular mortgage.

- You have a line of credit or a significant home equity line of credit. This can be an avenue—but of course, as with all flips, there are risks to using this. (Occasionally, you will hear of people using unsecured loans/money, like credit cards or a personal line of credit. Remember that nearly all flips will have at least a hiccup or two. This means choosing to risk your own personal credit—a chance you might not want to take.)

There are also rules related to Federal Housing Administration (FHA) loans and flips and renovations. In addition, conventional loans usually require more money down than a hard money lender—and again, they take longer. Your credit must also be very good to avoid issues coming up during the process. It's best to, again, seek the advice of your attorney and accountant to determine if conventional lending is right for you.

The Clock Is Ticking

Regardless of the type of financial arrangements you make, the moment you have money in hand and take possession of your property, the clock is ticking—from the minute the closing is complete. The longer you hold onto the property, the more interest you are paying.

So before you even bid on a house, you need to have your team (covered in letter *T*) lined up. Who is going to do the work? And are they ready to hit the ground running? I've closed on houses and have had work crews at the site within three hours of closing. The longer repairs take, the less profit you make day by day.

The moment you have money in hand and take possession of your property, the clock is ticking.

To avoid potentially having subcontractors who don't show up or who get held up on other jobs, causing their start date with you to falter, many house flippers have their own team that works only with them. This lets them start the minute the paperwork is signed and they have the keys.

Geographic Location

Location, location, location. We hear this phrase all the time—and never is it more appropriate than when talking about house flipping.

While obviously you can flip homes in your hometown, no matter where that is, flipping in hot markets or near cities and development or vacation spots will likely be more profitable. We'll also discuss rentals and Airbnbs in this chapter.

Hot Spots and Airbnbs

Location, in terms of touristy places or flips in beach areas, is important. Once you select a locale, then consider what people who visit that location are seeking. For example, in beach towns, you will see terms for houses like *ocean view, ocean front, ocean side, first line, second line,* etc. Obviously, those spots nearer the water are going to fetch the highest price, whether as a purchase, a rental, or an Airbnb. In a mountainous region, homes near ski resorts are desirable. In exciting towns like Austin or Nashville, people might want to be able to walk to nightlife.

Spots nearer the water are going to fetch the highest price, whether as a purchase, a rental, or an Airbnb.

Airbnb can be a great choice for house flippers in trendy areas. Airbnbs are popular with flippers who hold onto properties because, if it's in a good location, a week of Airbnb rentals will match a month of rent in a traditional year lease.

Airbnb potentials include places like Orlando, near Disney World, or other locations with amusement parks and tourist spots. Cities that are popular travel destinations are also ripe with Airbnb potential. Cities like Austin, Chicago, Boston, New York City, San Francisco, and locales with beautiful natural offerings—like Telluride, Park City, and Big Sur—are also ideal spots for Airbnbs. However, do your homework—some places are passing ordinances to try to limit the numbers of Airbnbs versus straight rentals, as residents complain of a lack of rental properties—and too many people in and out of homes or parties, etc.

Long-Distance Flipping

Is it possible to flip and have properties long distances from where you live?

You live in Maryland in a town far from any major tourist area. You are a fan of Nashville and see a great deal of Airbnb potential there. Can you flip a house long distance?

First, you need a good management company—one you trust. If you don't, you may find yourself using up your frequent flier miles going to your property to deal with issues like damage, plumbing leaks, and other surprises that can come up. (And trust me, they do.)

I would also not recommend long distance for your *first* flip. You need to get your feet wet with a hands-on project so you can go through the process yourself, to see all the details and ins and outs you will need to be ultimately responsible for. Plus, every single project will have something that goes wrong. It could be very minor—or it could be very complicated. Sorting out a major issue on your first flip while far from the property is less than ideal.

Just as you can hire crews for a flip in your own backyard, you can hire crews in a town three hours or a state away. However, remember that without a track record or a good broker or management company that might introduce you to people in the chosen town where you are flipping, it can be difficult to ensure that your crews, and all the work that needs to be done, line up just so without you there to supervise.

We once did a flip in Hawaii, thinking the location was worth it to attempt this long distance. Who doesn't love the exotic waters and tropical climate of the Big Island? However, with the time difference, for example, crews were working there during the day while it was evening where we were. Then when we flew there near completion and checked on the work, the walls were done incorrectly—and the barn door we chose was installed completely wrong. The cost of fixing these things behind the original crew was expensive—lesson learned.

Also keep in mind that luxe locations may lean more toward luxury flips, so the entry point for purchasing property is going to be higher (and distressed properties may be harder to find).

The Burbs

Location, location—schools, jobs, and neighborhoods. For those flipping in the suburbs versus the city, consider the elements suburban house buyers are most concerned about (and those you should be concerned about when choosing a geographic location for a suburban flip):

- Safety. Is the crime rate low? If there is a downtown area, is it well lit? Is there parking?

- Are there jobs nearby? Right now, giants like Tesla and Google and Amazon are choosing various locations in the country to expand. This immediately makes houses in those areas more valuable as thousands of people are hired or relocate. Not to mention, when big companies come to settle in an area, so do other businesses. Restaurants, shops, gyms, and grocery stores often follow to support the influx of people.

- Getting around. Is there safe public transportation? Are there enough roads and highways to make getting to work accessible and not a nightmare, bumper-to-bumper commute? Does the community have bike paths and sidewalks? Is the town walkable? Is there mixed-use development?

- Entertainment and restaurants. Suburban residents want access to trendy restaurants, family restaurants, and entertainment—whether that is a wine bar or movie theaters and concert halls. An isolated suburb that doesn't offer these things is not appealing.

- Schools. Do the schools have good test scores? Are they nearby? Are there enough schools relative to the populace so that they are not overcrowded?

- Culture. Are there nearby museums, parks, universities?

THE CIRCLE OF DESIRABILITY

When choosing a location, look at it as the center of concentric circles. In the center is the city, the popular suburb, the location that is most desirable. If a midsize city is safe and offers culture, entertainment and an attractive downtown, condos, homes, townhomes, and rentals in that area are going to be the green area—the most expensive and the most desirable.

The second layer is yellow. This is still close to the city—but not considered *in* it. There might be a short drive to jobs or to downtown entertainment. The houses may be a little less expensive—but they're still desirable. As cities grow, these houses will increase in value as people need housing close to the center—but there are only so many units that will ever be available in the green layer as a function of land, city crowding, etc.—so yellow becomes more desirable. You can see this phenomenon in so-called bedroom communities that are commutable from cities like New York. In places like the New York metropolitan area, LA, and the San Francisco Bay Area, commutes of ninety minutes one way or more are not unheard of. (Though with more hybrid work situations, this is shifting somewhat.)

The red layer is further out. Less convenient to work, to the downtown, less a part of the action and energy of downtown, the red layer likely offers fewer stores, restaurants, etc. There may be more sprawl or disorganized land development. These properties will cost less—but they also won't sell as fast.

COMMERCIAL REAL ESTATE: A QUICK WORD ON LOCATION

Some of the people reading this book are going to go on in their real estate investment career to perhaps enter the commercial real estate market. I would be remiss if I did not at least mention location and commercial real estate.

When Tesla's investment in Austin is complete, there could be an addition of up to twenty thousand jobs and billions of dollars poured into the local economy.[16] Every time a giant—Google, Amazon, Meta—or a midsize company builds or expands facilities in a new place, those people need housing as well as commercial development, like medical offices and strip malls/shopping, for example.

Austin already does not have enough housing inventory for the people who want to buy there. In this situation, moving into commercial real estate—apartments, condos, etc.—can be a lucrative opportunity, as multiunits help alleviate the housing crunch. Multifamily units (and mixed-use commercial properties) are an avenue to consider when entering real estate investing.

Raleigh-Durham, Nashville, Seattle, Boston, Charlotte—these are but a few of the markets where real estate investing is hot.

Home Inspection

You will have two home inspections for every house you flip. The first when you buy it; the second when you sell it.

First and foremost, don't be pressured into buying a house without the inspection. In very hot markets, there will be that pressure—I promise you. But it's rarely worth it. Learn from me: I once bought on the spot—and the house sure looked like a find. But there were significant foundation problems that were not readily visible as I toured the house. Though I turned a profit on the house, it was much less than I should have.

Your Home Inspection Company

You want to find a good home inspection company that you trust and that is thorough. This is a true story: I found the one I used when I was flipping houses because we had a house on the market. We are scrupulously honest, so I did not think the house had any issues now that we had flipped/remodeled it. Our own home inspector had not found anything. But the buyer's inspection company came, and they were so unbelievably thorough that they found issues our original home inspector never even thought of. We switched home inspection companies and worked with this new company until we stopped flipping and scaled our business.

Find a good home inspection company that you trust and that is thorough.

According to the American Society of Home Inspectors, these are the main things your home inspector checks:[17]

1. Heating system

2. Central air conditioning system (HVAC)

3. Interior plumbing and electrical systems

4. Roof and rain gutters

5. Attic, including visible insulation, leaks or past leaks, etc.

6. Walls

7. Ceilings

8. Floors

9. Windows and doors

10. Foundation

11. Basement

12. Structural components

13. Checks for insects

14. Major kitchen appliances

The inspector will note age, wear and tear, working condition, damage, etc. Inspections will never be foolproof. There are things hidden behind walls, in wiring, etc. that may not come up until you knock down a wall, for example. How many home improvement shows have you seen where everything is going swimmingly—until they knock down a wall and discover the wiring has been eaten by squirrels or some other crazy problem that will now cost the homeowner thousands more dollars?

In other words, you want to be as thorough as possible.

Buyer Beware

In **C: Choose Wisely**, I covered some of the important things to look for when choosing a house. In terms of the home inspection, there are some "biggies" that you should beware of and likely walk away from a house if these come up.

THE SELLER'S DISCLOSURE

A seller's disclosure form varies from state to state. However, the purpose of these is to alert the buyer to big or important issues and disclose any significant problems. If you know you have termite damage and do not disclose it, for example, the buyer can pursue you (a.k.a. sue you!) for the costs associated with getting rid of the problem.

Again, these vary from state to state, but here are some of the things that typically must be disclosed:

- Lead paint and other hazards. Older homes/historic homes may have lead paint left over from an era in which this type of paint was (unsafely) used. Lead has been linked to health and safety issues, including brain damage in children. A seller must disclose if lead paint has been used. This is a *federal* law for any home built earlier than 1978. Other hazards include asbestos, radon, and certain kinds of outdated insulation.

- Water damage.

- Nuisance neighbors—in some states this can mean foul odors (such as needing to disclose if a pig farm or major factory or oil refinery is nearby), landfills, shooting ranges, and if the airport nearby means fifteen 747s fly over your house each day.

- Major repairs. Some states require you to let the buyer know if you've previously fixed the foundation or if there was a sinkhole or some other issue requiring a significant repair.

- What comes with the house—and what doesn't. You may tour a house with a refrigerator or other items (chandeliers, smart-home accessories, etc.). Many states require that the seller list anything that does *not* come with the house (for example, some states *require* a refrigerator to convey to the new owner; others do not).

- Homeowner association information. The seller must make information on the homeowner association available to the buyer (including whether major assessments are coming up).

Analyze the Home Yourself

When you go to look at a home to potentially flip, you should have your own list of things to inspect and consider so you don't waste your time moving forward only to discover too much is wrong with the house. I used a checklist—and that checklist also helped me do some fast calculations on how much work there was to be done. (Remember your 70 Percent Rule.)

THE 70 PERCENT RULE

Most home flippers use the 70 Percent Rule to determine whether to purchase a home. This is the estimated value of the house after repairs are made as well as the estimated repair costs using this simple formula:

After-repair value (ARV) × 0.70 – Estimated repair costs = Maximum buying price

My checklist is set in table 1.

⊘	ITEM	Acceptable or Work Needed	Estimated Cost of Repair/ Replacement
	House insurance		
	Utilities		
	Remote door lock*		
	Foundation repair		
	Hydrostatic test**		
	Roof condition		
	Kitchen cabinets		

✓	ITEM	Acceptable or Work Needed	Estimated Cost of Repair/ Replacement
	Countertops—granite		
	Kitchen backsplash		
	Trash disposal		
	Garage door		
	Garage door openers		
	Yard fencing		
	AC units		
	Hot water tank or water heater		
	Window installation		
	Interior doors		
	Front door		
	Back door		
	Flooring		
	Tile bath floor		
	Tile bath walls		
	Bathtub(s)		
	Commodes		
	Vanities		
	Backsplash for vanity		
	Bath fixtures		
	Sink fixtures		

⊘	ITEM	Acceptable or Work Needed	Estimated Cost of Repair/ Replacement
	Shower fixtures		
	Shower floor tile		
	Dishwasher		
	Microwave		
	Range		
	Paint (walls, fireplace)		
	Paint, ceiling		
	Paint, outside		
	Paint, trim		
	Grout		
	Lights, standard		
	Lights, chandelier		
	Lights, wall mount		
	Lights, outside		
	Ceiling fans		
	Vanity lights		
	Mirrors		
	Baseboard		
	Doorknobs		
	Cabinet knobs		
	Plumbing repairs		

✓	ITEM	Acceptable or Work Needed	Estimated Cost of Repair/ Replacement
	Lawn service		
	Fireplace mantel/ design		
	Sheetrock/texture		
	Misc:		
	Labor hours, estimated		
* We put these on all our homes. They are very convenient. ** These tests check for drainpipes (leaks, etc.)			

Here are a couple of things you probably want to have as a flipper when you are going to look at houses:

- A moisture meter. Moisture meters can check the moisture level in drywall, wood, paneling, etc. There are different types (pin and pinless). Subcontractors may use them to check if, for example, wood is dry enough to paint. In terms of the home inspection, though, you are looking for moisture related to leaks.

- Zip level or other foundation-measuring tool. You might bring along a device that measures if the foundation is level or has shifted. However, when you are touring the house, you should be doing a visual inspection. Look for obvious cracks on the walls (especially deep ones that do not appear to be related to paint or wear and tear).

- Infrared thermometer for temperature differential checks of air conditioning. An air conditioner is an expensive item, so making sure it runs well is a check you can perform when touring a house with your broker. Note—it is more difficult to test an air conditioner when it is cold out—so keep that in mind if you purchase in winter in a hot-climate locale.

Inventory

The inventory of houses fluctuates with the market and the economy. How can you tell if a market has inventory or if inventory is tight? How is it measured? To me, average or normal market conditions mean there are six months of inventory. In other words, there is enough housing to buy for the next six months for people who wish to move into the area or move from one house to another in the area.

One of the country's hot markets might have less than a month of inventory (always subject to change as market conditions shift). There are more people that want houses (many more) than there are houses to purchase.

Hot and cold markets are part of real estate. There are trends as well. Sometimes, there is a strong migration south, such as to states like Florida. There are, for many people, tax benefits to moving to Florida, which has a generous homestead exemption, for example (which protects someone's primary residence from levies through judgments). Other cost-of-living factors in the South tend to be lower than large cities in the Northeast or on the West Coast, for example. So it's attractive for retirees. Arizona is another market retirees like— the warm weather is definitely a plus as well.

At the same time, some markets cool. The difficulties during the global COVID-19 pandemic, for example, had many people fleeing New York City. One of the attractive things about living in New York City (and other large cities) is the cultural offerings. New York City is a mecca for foodies, for example. It offers world-class museums like the Metropolitan Museum of Art and the Museum of Modern Art. But during the global COVID-19 pandemic, restaurants shuttered and museums were closed. New York apartment dwellers, stuck working virtually from kitchen tables or small bedrooms, sought a haven upstate or out on Long Island or out of the area entirely.

Another big factor in hot markets can occur when a large corporation relocates or opens a large facility in a new location. Companies like Samsung, Tesla, Disney, Google, or Amazon, by virtue of the sheer number of jobs and employees they have, can create a boom if they move into a new area.

When there is not a lot of housing inventory, it obviously drives the prices higher. It also makes *your* job as investor or house flipper a little more difficult. (Even though it can be very lucrative.) The competition for those undervalued properties is more intense. So what does a house flipper do to find their inventory?

First, while the MLS (the Multiple Listing Service that real estate agents utilize) is a powerful tool, if you are a real estate investor, you are not just going to be looking for your inventory on that MLS, which is where everybody is looking. Ideally, you would love to find undervalued properties before they even hit the market.

For most people, that is going to mean having wholesaler connections (which we will cover more completely in **W: Wholesalers**). That will necessitate networking so that those wholesalers reach out to you and vice versa. We'll get to that in a bit.

The Cold Call

Let's begin with a technique that new flippers are often advised to use. If you are just starting, you may wish to act as your own wholesaler. How can you do that? You may go out driving in neighborhoods that are ripe for flipping. You should be studying your chosen area carefully.

- Look for a lot of sales activity. This can mean this is a hot neighborhood or that the school system or proximity to stores and entertainment makes it desirable. It could also mean a good commutable distance from a city or a major employer.

- Pay attention to the ages of homes. You need to be cautious of *very* old homes that are seventy and eighty years old (and older). Building materials used back then may not be up to code or need replacing. A home that is more recent but old enough to need updating is ideal. You want a home with good bones and sound structure but in which upgrades may make that older home shine. In addition, older homes may, in turn, have older owners ready to downsize. Since they have likely paid off their home (or have more equity in them than one owned by a young family), they may be more flexible on price. Sometimes, older homes might be sold by the children or heirs of an older owner who has passed away. They are not interested in moving into the home—and are open to selling quickly without having to make a lot of updates.

- Seek out older charm. If you see newer developments of hundreds of homes, you are unlikely to find a bargain to flip (unless you find a home in foreclosure, but even then, you are not likely to see the kind of profit of a redone flipped home). But if you see neighborhoods with mostly charming old homes with quaint details, slow down and take a look.

- Narrow down your search to neighborhoods you think are prime for flipping. Then drive through. Look for homes that haven't been updated or may look a little run down. Now is the time to cold call. Knock on doors and introduce yourself. Leave your card, direct them to your website, etc. (For safety reasons, I suggest always working with a partner on these calls.)

Here's a real-life example from my house-flipping business. I was driving through neighborhoods looking for properties and analyzing areas. I passed an older home. It was not in a terrible state of disrepair, but it definitely needed some TLC. As I drove by, I saw a thirtysomething man getting rid of a lot of stuff in the garage, tossing boxes and items into one of those large dumpsters people rent to dispose of a bunch of junk at once. That was definitely a sign. The dumpster was *full* of stuff. I stopped and spoke with him. He was selling his dad's home; his father had passed away six months before. This guy really did not want to have to paint and repair and do everything necessary to put the house on the market and stage it. His father had left a lot of clutter behind. The son was just cleaning out the house to make it look somehow presentable to put it on the market. I asked if my contractor and I could take a look. The man said yes, and I called my contractor—who luckily was maybe ten miles away (lucky, because you must move fast on a potential find). The man's late father had been the original owner, but he hadn't painted or done any repair work in years. The house had some strange odors and was very dark and dingy inside. After thoroughly looking around, examining the foundation, etc., I made a cash offer on the spot, which the son was very grateful for. Not only did a cash offer avoid contingencies, etc., but it was a fast closing. Since he was from out of town, this suited him even more. This ended up being a very successful flip for me—the house, under all that gloominess, became a very attractive property with new landscaping, including cutting down a dead tree up front, new living room and primary bedroom windows that let in much more light, new flooring in the kitchen, new stainless appliances, and new paint. I also redid the bathrooms with new vanities and custom mirrors and knocked down a wall separating the kitchen from the dining room.

I did want to mention something—especially if you are new to flipping. You would not think it's much—but sometimes homes are so full of junk that hauling it away is a significant expense. So don't forget things like that when you calculate your potential profit. You might negotiate in the contract for the seller to handle the removal of the junk—or you might take a bit off your offer price to accommodate that expense.

One more thing about this particular flip is that this man was so grateful that he didn't have to do all that work (which would have been expensive, let alone the fact that he did not have experience in real estate—he was a middle school teacher in Seattle and certainly preferred not having to spend his whole summer dealing with his dad's house). The *buyers* were thrilled too. They were a young couple with a new baby—and the neighborhood was perfect for them. Both sides of this deal were happy with the outcome, which in turn made me feel great about what I was able to do.

Wholesalers

One thing that may be very surprising to you if you start flipping in a hot market is that inventory can be so tight that houses may sell in less than a day—houses that are in terrible shape. I've seen cases where sellers are listing a house without even attaching pictures because it is an as-is house and someone will take it without even seeing anything more. In addition, as I discuss in **G: Geographic Location,** in a hot market, people from out of state and investors who are working from a distance can snap things up from wholesalers.

We will, as I said, address wholesalers more fully later, but for now, know if you plan to be a flipper as more than a hobby (i.e., doing multiple projects, not just one or two houses a year), wholesalers will be crucial to your business. One reason is that someone *else* (someone well connected/networked in finding properties) will be locating houses for you to buy—leaving you to run your flipping business. If you plug the term "off-market properties" into any search engine, wholesale listing websites and companies will be the top results.

Get on social media to look for wholesalers and brokers you can rely on.

Once you choose the area where you are going to be flipping properties, it is time to get on social media to look for wholesalers and brokers you can rely on. You want trustworthy people and companies—and that will mean reading about their reputations online, as well as networking yourself and seeing if you can find people who have had dealings with them. I don't think any successful real estate investor or house flipper is without a story of some negative real estate transaction—whether bad contracts or real estate agents who inflate properties beyond what is reasonable.

Once you find a couple of reliable and trustworthy wholesalers to work with, it is the best situation. Every single day you will be getting emails with available properties. You need to act quickly. Also keep in mind if you are purchasing properties long distance, you will want to have someone who works with you to take a fast look.

In addition, even if working with a wholesaler, you still need to be very careful to read all the contracts and paperwork (having a good lawyer is important, especially in the beginning when you may not know what to look for). Sometimes off-market properties have contingencies. I had one such problem with a property in which there was a contingency that the seller could remain in the property until they found and bought their next home. They extended the closing date first one month, then two, and finally three months—which was three months of lost time. Just because someone is a wholesaler does not mean the properties have been vetted for problems. Do your due diligence.

Auctions

You might consider finding a house at auction. Where I live, I can go online on the first Tuesday of the month and find a listing of all the properties that are going to be auctioned that month. Investors often choose auctions because there can be real bargains (minimum opening bids that are much lower than market rate) to be had. But as in all real estate investing, there are cautions and considerations:

- Drive by the property. Are there obvious big-ticket repairs needed, like a cracked foundation? With an auction, you will not be allowed inside to tour the home. You must assess the outside as much as possible.

- Go to the neighborhood at different times of day and after dark to see how safe it feels. Are there many commuters, young families, single people? Look up the school system if it's a neighborhood for young families. It's up to you to learn as much as possible about the community.

- Know there are different kinds of auctions, depending on the county and state you live in. Some are reserve auctions (meaning the bids are treated almost like regular buyer's bids—so if there are multiple bids, the seller can go through and pick and weigh them all and then make a decision). Others might have a minimum bid. If you are going to try to buy properties at auction, it's helpful to know about the different kinds of auctions. (I discovered in Texas sometimes investors literally draw straws in some areas.)

- You are buying the property as is. Buyer beware. Remember that auction sales are as-is sales—so if you buy the house and it turns out it needs more work than you thought … too bad.

- Come ready to pay cash or have your financing in order. You cannot buy a house at auction and then go and find your financing. You must be prepared before you even bid.

- You may find unpleasant surprises. One of the problems with auctions is that the seller does not have to disclose things the way they would if it was a regular house sale. This is beyond the property needing repairs. There could be liens on the house or complicating issues that have to do with the financial side that you need to look into (for example, if a homeowner association has a significant lien on the home, you would need to pay that off—but legally you do not have to be told about this ahead of time in an auction situation).

Yellow Letters

Some flippers can find their properties using what's termed *yellow letters*. You may have even received one of these. Yellow letters look handwritten (even though they are computer-generated). It is a direct appeal to the homeowner. It can be as simple as this:

Dear Homeowner: My name is _____. I would like to buy your house at [INSERT ADDRESS]. I am familiar with your neighborhood and would love a chance to speak to you. Please contact me at _____.

These direct mail pieces can be sent in bulk. You can find all sorts of statistics on the response rate for direct mail pieces with some citing as low as 1 percent and as high as 7 percent or more. The fact is direct mail campaigns are a numbers game. Send enough and you will get a response—and may just find an undervalued property where an owner is receptive to speaking with you and hearing what you have to offer.

Also be aware that, if you aspire to grow your investing business to eventually work in commercial properties, yellow letters won't work there. They are strictly for residents of neighborhoods.

Other Ways to Find Inventory

Depending on where you live in the country, you will see all sorts of creative ways to find properties. These can include the following:

- Billboards
- Bus and transportation benches
- Radio and television commercials

- Calling all for-sale-by-owner properties and gauging how motivated they are (and making an offer based on that)

- Bandit signs (small signs that list your phone number with "We pay cash for houses" or some similar verbiage)

Judgments and Foreclosures

In **I: Inventory** we discuss auctions and creative ways to find properties. Judgments and foreclosures are also definitely part of finding distressed properties for investment.

Here's the first rule of finding a home in judgment or foreclosure: The further away you get from the original owner, the more likely there is not a clear title. In other words, once a bank or another entity has taken possession of the home, as opposed to the person who once owned the house, the more likely it is that there could be liens or other hidden issues.

If a house is in foreclosure or going into foreclosure and you are interested in it, the best thing you can do for yourself is to find that owner, whoever it is, and just deal with them directly. This may mean you are not dealing with a wholesaler, even.

In addition, know that you may not be able to inspect the property. Is there water damage in the basement? Are there plumbing issues? Do expensive things need to be replaced? You usually can't tell from the outside. But what *can* you determine from a drive past? Are there significant cracks in the foundation? How much landscaping needs to be done? Does the roof look decrepit? Will a fence need replacing?

For some investors, foreclosures are a good way to buy houses.

However, for some investors, foreclosures are a good way to buy houses. Now, obviously, it is very sad that someone, perhaps through a job loss or a change in circumstances, is now in a foreclosure proceeding. However, and especially if a home is in preforeclosure, it can be a big relief for them to be rid of that mortgage hanging over them. So sometimes it is something that benefits both you and the beleaguered homeowner. You get a house to flip; they are freed from onerous payments.

The best way to find houses for foreclosures is to go on county websites and official websites, where they list all those houses. You can find some listings through the Department of Housing and Urban Development (on HUD.gov) when the government is now the lender and the home is in foreclosure. There are also websites that list properties from all over the United States (such as www.auction.com). You can even sign up for a subscription to a foreclosure listing service that gathers and sends the listings—you can go through that list all at once instead of having to hunt through a variety of sources. Depending on where you live, there could be dozens or even hundreds of listings. These listings will provide the name, phone number, and email of the person you need to contact (though with foreclosed properties, there are often twists and turns in who actually is authorized to sell the property). Now, remember, if you are paying for a subscription, so are a lot of other investors. Be prepared to move quickly—which is always important in flipping houses.

Some banks maintain their own lists of properties in foreclosure. Most banks want market price. If the home is in severe disrepair, it may be below market. *Market price* means average—the bank is just looking to get rid of the house. They don't want to give it away—but they aren't pricing it as high as a real estate agent, etc. Banks are not in the real estate business—well, they are. They finance mortgages. But they don't want an inventory of foreclosed-on properties that may be losing value through neglect. Making an offer at market value might be fruitful for you.

Take special notice if you discover a home is in preforeclosure. That term means that payments were not made. The bank has likely sent several (or more!) notices. The homeowner might be struggling to figure out a solution. If the house is purchased, though—and the new buyer pays off the belated payments—then the seller doesn't lose all their home equity to the foreclosure by giving up the home entirely. You, as the flipper, are coming in at just the right time to get the house before it is tied up in the complexities and paperwork for a bank or lender foreclosure on the property.

Sometimes you may hear of wraparound closings or mortgages. I do not recommend this type of gamble—but you should be aware of it if someone suggests it. The simplest way to describe it is the investor is paying for the mortgage. Eventually the title is transferred—but there are tax implications and also a higher chance that something can go wrong with the arrangement. This is always the risk with unconventional financing. People who are perhaps desperate may make decisions they would not if they were thinking clearheadedly.

I will also add that some of these strategies simply will not work in a hot market. There is not time for the more creative financing strategies. There are too many investors with cash in hand.

Finally, you may find a house in foreclosure through brokers you work with. Real estate agents are often very knowledgeable about the neighborhoods where they have listings. Very often, for example, you will find a housing development or neighborhood where nearly everyone who lists their home for sale uses the same real estate agency. The agent may live in that neighborhood or have expertise and knowledge (as well as interested buyers). Through their network and people they know, brokers may hear about a home in preforeclosure before it is listed on a website.

Knowledge

With home renovation shows and magazines, online before-and-afters, etc., it can look (deceptively) like house flipping is easy. Because so many of those shows and articles are based on the design wow factor of transforming an ugly space into a beautiful one, it can seem as if that is the bulk of the job of a house flipper.

Of course, nothing could be further from the truth. In fact, though paint colors and finishes and staging are important in showing off your hard work, so much of house flipping is in the other details—how to pull out old bathtubs (and check for water damage), checking that the ceiling lines where sheetrock has been put up are straight and clean—making sure, in short, all the construction details are right.

So if you want to become knowledgeable about house flipping, where do you begin? First, before you seek out knowledge and study, etc., you will want to ask yourself some questions about your real estate investment goals:

1. Do you have your finances ready? If you are working with all cash, then this applies a little less to you (but you would still need that cash to be liquid assets, able to be accessed quickly). However, to be a successful house flipper, you are going to need cash flow, and you are going to need to know how you are financing (Conventional loans? Partnerships?).

2. How handy are you? Some people get into house flipping because they enjoy DIY projects. Maybe you've transformed your own fixer-upper house and now want to try a house flipping project. Maybe you're a subcontractor who has done some kitchen remodels and feel ready to tackle a whole house for your own business. Or maybe you are an investor with a good eye for design. Before you knock down that first wall, make sure you have an *honest* assessment of your own skills and what you *can* do and what you *want* to do. Because outside of that, you will have to hire people.

3. Do you have a team? Maybe you are supplying the financing and your partner is a contractor who is going to do most of the heavy lifting. Perhaps, like my company, you are the brains behind the company and finding properties—and you've assembled a great team of other brains, each of them with their own expertise. Your team might include contractors and sub-

You want to surround yourself with people who have the skills and knowledge you don't.

contractors, plumbers, painters, roofers, etc. (We will get into all the different team members in **T: Team**.) You will for sure need a real estate attorney, perhaps wholesalers, etc. You need this team lined up first before you do much of anything else. Especially in hot markets, talented people are in demand. You want to surround yourself with people who have the skills and knowledge you don't.

4. What kind of investing do you want to do? Single-family homes? Multifamily? Commercial? Do you want to buy properties for Airbnbs or rentals? In short, what kind of flipper do you want to be? Are you going to hold onto a portfolio or flip as fast as you can? What kind of time frame are you working with? Once you narrow down what you want to do, then you can learn as much as possible in that area.

I am sure you have seen or heard commercials for people who will teach you the house-flipping business. They are courses where you will do most of the legwork—and in return, you will learn the ins and outs of house flipping and real estate investment. Some of these courses are excellent—like anything, you want to do your due diligence. Read reviews and learn what you can about the people teaching it. Some are franchises, so you should be able to find out more from former students online.

Some colleges offer extension classes (continuing study classes) for certificates in various aspects of real estate investment. For example, Harvard offers a real estate investment graduate certificate. These college courses can be online, in person, or a combination/hybrid class.

You can also partner with an experienced house flipper to learn the ropes. You might bring the investment money, and your partner for the house might bring the know-how. Or vice versa. It can be a little difficult to find a partner when starting out—until you have developed your brand, name recognition, and reputation. Nonetheless, you should be talking to house flippers through networking and contacts—and learning from someone who has done this a dozen times or for a few years is the best on-the-job education.

You can also get an education via obtaining a contractor's license. Every state has different requirements to be a contractor (of course they do—why make it less complicated?). You might pursue this because you want to be very involved in the demo and remodeling, or you want to do some of the work yourself, or you simply want a very solid base of knowledge so you can judge how well the work on your property is being done.

Getting a contractor's license will also teach you some of the purely business aspects of remodeling a house. What licenses and permits do you need? You can learn about how to structure a contracting business, for example. If you do not have a lot of experience with the red tape of running a business, a contracting licensure can teach you some of that.

In addition, most contracting licensure classes (again, depending on the state) will teach you, or offer additional certifications, in the main areas of working on a house:

- HVAC

- Plumbing

- Flooring

- Roofing

- Safety codes

- Blueprint reading

Knowledge of all these areas can be very helpful to you. It can save you money if you can act as your own contractor as opposed to hiring one, it can help you assess the work of others, and it can give you the kind of broad knowledge of the business that is beneficial.

Do you want to be a **B: Broker** as part of your education? There are pluses and minuses to getting a broker's license, which you can read about in letter *B*. Getting a license will give you more than access to the MLS. It can give you a base of knowledge in financing and contracts. Again, it is not necessary (and is more focused on the fine-print aspects of real estate), but it can give you another avenue of knowledge of the business.

Leads

Without leads you cannot be in the house-flipping business. If you don't find a house to flip—you have no product!

There are different approaches to developing and finding leads, depending on what stage you are at. You might be starting on your first house; you might have a couple under your belt; you might be very seasoned and about to take your company to the next level.

One approach, especially if you are new, is the cold call. I discuss this in detail in **I: Inventory**, including a story of how I found a great investment house by approaching a man cleaning out a garage on a house in a state of disrepair. I noticed he was cleaning out the house because his father had passed away. Within forty-eight hours, I had bought the house, paying cash, and this man was saved from having to haul away all the junk and painting and repairing the house to make it showable.

As I pointed out in that entry, there are many lists you can sign up for, from wholesalers to others, that will let you know about properties in preforeclosure and foreclosure. Just remember that a listing might be one house—with many people/entities receiving this list. So it is important to remember—as with anything in house flipping—that speed is of the essence. I don't want to give the impression that you should make decisions too quickly, ignoring your due diligence and homework. However, you need to be aware that in the world of house flipping, the clock is always ticking.

Since we have covered many aspects of building your inventory through leads in **I: Inventory,** let's look at what happens when you find a lead. These are the steps I recommend to organize and track your leads.

Typical Lead Processing

Here are some steps for conducting an interview:

1. Create a profile form (this is the basics: name, address, phone, email, etc.).

2. Determine the situation (Is the person looking to sell a distressed property, are they in foreclosure, etc.?).

3. Analyze the numbers (Does this property even make sense through the 70 Percent Rule, or is it a property that will not work with the current financials?).

4. Discuss options (What are the options for taking on the property?).

THE 70 PERCENT RULE

Most home flippers use the 70 Percent Rule to determine whether to purchase a home. This is the estimated value of the house after repairs are made as well as the estimated repair costs using this simple formula:

After-repair value (ARV) × 0.70 – Estimated repair costs = Maximum buying price

The questions I recommend asking are shown in the following figure, "Lead Sheet."

Finally, **L: Leads** and **M: Marketing** are interrelated—fortunately they are right next to each other in the alphabet, so read on.

LEAD SHEET

1. Name

2. Phone

3. Second phone number

4. Email

5. Address

6. Estimated value

7. Square feet of the home

8. The number of bedrooms and bathrooms

9. Do you need to buy another home? Or is this sale independent of that?

10. Property type (Single-family house? Townhome? Multifamily house, etc.)

11. Garage

12. Pool (What is the state of the pool?)

13. Who lives in the home? Who am I going to be dealing with?

14. Approximate first mortgage payoff

15. Approximate second mortgage payoff

16. Lot size

17. Estimated repairs, remodeling

18. Total monthly payment

19. Approximate last payment made

20. Approximate year home built

21. Listed with real estate agent?

22. Back taxes owed?

23. Is there a homeowner association? Is the homeowner current with their payments?

24. Reasons for sale

25. How quickly do you need to sell?

26. Loan lender?

27. What are the names on the deed?

DEALS TO AVOID:

1. Mobile homes

2. No equity on home or someone on deed missing/left town or dead

3. Homeowners just declared bankruptcy

4. Private loans (they rarely work)

5. Suspected mortgage fraud

6. Secondary liens

Calculate your bid/offer.

Map your strategy.

Close the deal.

M

Marketing

There are numerous ways to market your entity/company and your house-flipping business. Marketing is important to get your name out there, not only to attract business but also to help build your team. In a crowded house-flipping market where finding excellent contractors or wholesalers is paramount, if you are very new, it can be hard to make those connections. Marketing helps you establish your presence in the area in which you wish to do business.

We all know what marketing looks like (Google ads, TV ads, brochures and print media, billboards, door hangers, etc.). But what is marketing's purpose? Marketing is a form of communication. It lets the public, the people you are aiming to market to, know who you are and what you do. It delivers a message. Therefore it is essential that your message and marketing be as professional as possible. Marketing directly impacts the perception of your entity.

Let's look at some ways to market your real estate ventures.

Your Website

In **E: Entity**, we covered establishing your brand. Your company name should be easy to look up online. In other words, do not choose names with hyphens, homophones (words like *to*, *too*, *two*), or difficult-to-spell words. So if your last name is very unusual, it is likely best that you avoid using your name as your realty company and web domain.

Your website is your "home" on the internet. Just as you stage your properties, you will want the essence of your website to showcase you best. It should be professional, clean, and uncluttered and should be easy to navigate. If you are displaying before-and-after images of some of the properties you have flipped, be sure they are "Instagram-worthy" and professional.

Make your website copy sing. If you are posting before-and-afters, "sell" the house (even if it's already sold!). Talk about the shiny new appliances and the redone bathrooms; describe the property and the neighborhood in glowing terms. Make sure you use search engine optimization (SEO) terms so that people find you on the internet.

You might also consider giving something away on your website. This could be as simple as a very short e-book on *20 Best Ways to Stage Your Home* or an informational workbook for investors.

Social Media

I cover this topic more fully in **S: Social Media**, but obviously, if you are doing real estate, you need a social media footprint. Facebook, LinkedIn, Twitter, and Instagram are the four platforms that are most popular in the real estate business. In general, I advise this: Do not start a social media presence if you are not going to keep up with it. In other words, if you create a professional Facebook page and don't update it for a year, that is not even worth it—in fact, it may look like you went out of business. So if you are just starting out and you are not sure you can keep up with all the platforms, start with one and build from there.

Do not start a social media presence if you are not going to keep up with it.

Know that, increasingly, the algorithms on social media platforms favor video. So if you can do a before-and-after home tour on video or offer real estate or staging tips on video, do so. You can also investigate running ads on social media. A plus of today's data-driven market is that you can target ads to very specific categories. So, for example, if you want your ads seen by young, single professionals, you can do so. If you think the neighborhood you have chosen to focus on is ideal for retirees or for young families, you can focus your ads toward that demographic.

Go Local

If you are part of a community and are working at flipping in that community, you are in an ideal position to go local.

Going local means looking for marketing opportunities where you are located or working. Can you sponsor a Little League team? Can your brand be put on a banner at the local ball field? Can you sponsor a pizza lunch at the local elementary school for field day? You want to look for opportunities to be part of the fabric of the community where you are engaged.

If you are focusing on a certain area, make sure your website also includes local elements. For example, if you are a resident of Atlanta, your website menu can include an "About Atlanta" pulldown where you have links to all sorts of valuable and important websites someone relocating to Atlanta might need: the local utilities companies, museum links, links for local parks or tourist attractions, etc. You can also write articles or have a blog on local elements (or hire someone to).

Google Ads and Google Profiles

It is not enough to simply build a website and put it on the internet. You will want your Google business profile to be current, with hours, location, website link, photos, phone number, etc. It is imperative that this be up to date.

Google ads are also a marketing tool. I will tell you later in this entry about my experiences—suffice it to say, for now, that you should really do some homework on how to buy Google ads, what you are buying, and the costs. Google ad expenses can rise rapidly—and you may not see immediate returns. This is an area where learning all you can about how the ads work will help you.

Newsletters

It takes a while to build a legitimate email list. You *do not* want to buy email lists. There are, first of all, laws regarding spam. Even if the list is legitimate and has been carefully culled and vetted, when you send a newsletter this way, you will be perceived as a spammer.

However, organically building a newsletter list is terrific. There are some things to keep in mind:

- Newsletters can build engagement.

- Newsletters let you send content specific to the types of homes and real estate you are pursuing. You can personalize it as much as you want.

- Newsletters build traffic to your website and help build your brand.

- Make opting in to your newsletter easy in the signature of your email.

Business Cards and Presence

I know there are online templates to make business cards. However, it does not cost all that much to print higher-quality cards that reflect your presence. But make sure you are also building your presence using technology—QR codes, for example. Doorhangers are another item you could have printed up. You are trying to build a name people recognize.

Look for What Works with Your Goals

What are your house-flipping goals? Depending on what you want to achieve, there are other outside-the-box marketing ideas you can use. You could offer online virtual tours, or you could host a webinar in an area of your house-flipping/real estate investing expertise. You might decide to specialize in certain types of flips or houses. Perhaps you work in a certain community or you focus on townhomes. Whatever your specialty, you can market it according to the aspirations you have for the type of real estate you want to be involved with.

My Real-Life Marketing Story

I decided to promote my company, and I put a sign on an office building in town. I considered it an experiment because I really did not yet know what the right marketing approaches were going to be. I had faith in my brand/entity, and I wanted to see if this approach would work. It did. Within a week or two of advertising, I had ten significant leads. They were often people saying, "I saw your sign on *xyz* building, and I was wondering if you are still looking at investment properties."

On the flip side, when my company was just starting, we researched the quickest way to get leads—and many articles and other sources said it was Google ads. For real estate Google ads, your company pops up when someone searches, and people click on it and go to the website and call you because your number is there, your email is there—it is easy to find you (an absolute must for marketing). It seemed perfect.

In actuality, I think in a month of ads, we got a single decent lead. I kept with it (I am nothing if not stubborn!). My results were similar. Now, I have to offer a caveat that some people are very successful with Google ads and online ads in general. I ended up working with a much smaller online firm for ads—and did much better. You need to find an approach that works for your company.

When I was new to all this, I didn't fully understand online marketing as I do now. Google's Display Network means you can focus your ads to a geographic region, to personal interests, etc. Here's a partial list of Google's audience types to target:

- "Affinity: Reach users based on what they're passionate about and their habits and interests."

- "Custom Segments: Depending on your campaign goal, reach users based on what they're passionate about, their habits and interests. Also reach users based on their recent purchase intent."

- "Life Events: Reach users when they are in the midst of important life milestones." [18]

Affiliate Marketing

Affiliate marketing is a form of online marketing where blogs and websites mention your product. If someone makes a purchase via a link on that blog or website (cookies will track for a period of time, usually thirty days, but sometimes as much as ninety), the affiliate marketer makes a commission. If you have a website where you offer real estate advice and information and you get decent traffic, you can become an affiliate marketer (you can apply to various affiliate programs and see if you are accepted). This can lead to extra income. However, you can also purchase placements with affiliate marketers. I was fortunate in that my first flips were very successful, and I was rapidly so busy that I did not need to delve into this type of marketing. Amazon.com uses affiliate marketing extraordinarily successfully (not for real estate—yet!).

Bandit Ads

Many real estate investors use "bandit ads." You have probably seen them as you drive around whatever town you live in. Usually, these small signs say things like "We Pay Cash for Houses." It's important that these signs be very basic and clear and uncluttered. Placement is important too. If there is a neighborhood you'd like to invest in, planting these signs on the main thoroughfare into that development would be smart. However, every city, county, or local area likely has its own codes and regulations related to this. For example, a county may have a rule that the signs must be taken down after a set period. Or you may not be able to place the ad on certain highways. If you are caught violating the codes of your area, you can be fined.

Your Best Marketing is *You*!

At the heart of every marketing effort is your product. Your best marketing tools are houses and projects that are successful. You are building your brand, and all the parts of your marketing and networking ideas should be part of that. As we discuss in **E: Entity**, your name and look, your website and business cards, and any swag you give away should be professional.

If you advertise your company, the first thing a prospect is going to do is google you. If I can't find a website for a company, I immediately (fairly or not) think perhaps there is something shady about them.

You will never regret setting yourself up for success! I would rather spend the time at the outset of forming my company getting all this aligned than try to do it after the fact.

Yellow Letters

In **I: Inventory,** we cover yellow letters. These have the look of a handwritten letter and are a bulk mailing item. Like bandit ads, they are fairly straightforward.

"Dear _____: I am interested in buying your home at _____. Please call me at _____ so we can discuss."

I never needed to use yellow letters. However, as with all direct mail, it is a numbers game. You just need for your yellow letter to arrive in the right mailbox of someone looking to sell!

Timing Is Everything

When marketing, pay attention to seasons. In the United States, the strongest moving season is from May to September.[19] One reason is many people like to move in the summer so their kids can make friends in their new neighborhood before school starts in the fall. By the way, roughly forty million people move every year in the US.[20] (Think of all the houses they have to buy!)

Very few people move during the holiday season (I cannot even imagine packing up a house and moving during the holidays). Therefore, it goes without saying (but I will say it) that you should not be timing your marketing efforts at that time of year. It will be like throwing your money away. Plan your marketing campaigns with the best likelihood of success.

Plan your marketing campaigns with the best likelihood of success.

Pinpoint Your Targets; Track Your Results

One thing Google ads, affiliate marketing, and other marketing efforts do is force you to focus on your targets. In the beginning, you might be looking to find houses. But as your success builds, if you want to grow your company, you may want to find investors to partner with on projects. So how do you target those people? And then how do you track your results? It's important to be able to see what works and what doesn't. To do so, you will need to define your *metrics*. Did the campaign make a noticeable difference in traffic to your website? Did your yellow letter mailing result in six leads that resulted in you buying several of them?

You also need to know how to use the analytics that technology offers. If you are not comfortable with the newest technology, or you get so busy that it's difficult to keep up with that as well as your day-to-day house-flipping business, consider hiring a part-time person to help you with this. Most websites and online elements of marketing can tell you how many page views you received, how much time people spent on that page (and looking around your website), open rates for newsletters, bounce rates, and more.

Return on Your Marketing Investment

Finally, marketing is a fine line. As I've written here, I've included low-cost suggestions (for example, an online newsletter costs you time, if you do it yourself from a template, but not a lot of money) as well as marketing ideas that could run into the tens of thousands (a large Google ad campaign). You will need to weigh the return—which makes tracking your results even more important.

Networking

Networking is all about building contacts in your chosen field. No house flipper can do it all. Far from it. You need a strong **T: Team** to be successful. No one can buy, rehab, and sell a home—including all the physical work, as well as staging and marketing—all by themselves. Contacts are key.

When I was first starting out in flipping, I already knew that wholesalers and relationships with brokers were essential to my plan. Unfortunately, it is not like you can call up a wholesaler and expect that these people are going to jump to help you. They already have clients and people they work with. In a hot housing market, as another example, the *best* plumbers and drywall specialists, the best landscapers, etc. are not going to put off their existing clients to work with you. Thus, networking is so important.

In fact, I would say networking is more than essential. I remember watching a segment on TV with a prominent real estate developer who did a lot of commercial work. He had made a fortune in real estate investment. The journalist asked, "How many contacts do you have in your phone?" Playfully, he asked, "How many contacts do you think I have in my phone?" She said, "Oh, a couple of thousand." Then he smiled and said he had approximately fifteen thousand contacts.

Networking Events

Networking events for real estate agents or real estate investors can occur locally (especially if you are in a large suburb or midsize city). This might be a happy hour at a local restaurant or some other casual event. Once I got busy, I could not make as many of these events. However, I want to say that we located our real estate attorney at one of these events. Just one significant contact can mean setting you on your path if you are new to the house-flipping business. There are also very large real estate networking events held as conferences.

Chamber of Commerce and Other Professional Organizations

The Chamber of Commerce may offer great networking contacts in the community where you want to work. Not every place has a Chamber of Commerce, but most midsize and larger cities and counties have them. Your local chamber can offer a variety of events from basic monthly networking meetings to luncheons, happy hours, or other social events.

Your local chamber will have all sorts of businesses involved in it, from hair salons to restaurants to law and accounting professionals, as well as real estate people. Network with everyone (because you never know where a contact will lead), but focus on those who can help your house-flipping business—for example, lenders, or brokers or a well-regarded CPA.

Rotary clubs and other business organizations are also good networking opportunities. Rotary clubs are, in a nutshell, professional businesspersons coming together to do humanitarian work (whether local or broader). There are other professional organizations that can offer networking opportunities (and you may do good and have fun while doing so). Some target entrepreneurs. Others might be focused on female business owners and professionals, for example.

Start Local

Whatever community you are in, start locally. Network at shops and restaurants. Put up door hangers. Knock on those doors and introduce yourself. Get involved. As I discuss in **M: Marketing,** can you sponsor local teams or a sign at the ball park? How can you get your name out locally?

Very often, if you look around neighborhoods with for sale signs, you will see the same name(s) pop up over and over. A friend of mine's parents lived in a midsize planned community in Florida—and, with a few exceptions, one woman had listed most of the houses in certain neighborhoods. She lived in the community, knew its selling points, etc. When someone becomes an expert on a community, they become the first name people think of with their real estate needs. If you concentrate your flipping in certain neighborhoods, you will be trying to build your connections there, as well as building a name for yourself as someone who flips houses and makes them beautiful.

Online Networking

When I was a new house flipper/real estate investor, I made a point of joining quite a few Facebook groups. Some were for house flippers all over. Others focused in my area or state.

A few things to keep in mind when networking online:

Watch your tone. Sometimes a snarky comment that will work in person and make someone laugh can fall flat online. Just as you would stage a house you are trying to sell, the "staging" of your online social media profile is a look inside your company. Be positive; don't complain about market conditions. Don't badmouth competitors.

If you attend a virtual networking event, keep it professional.

Engage. It is not enough to slap up a profile and not nurture it. Make connections, share content, *create* content. If you are using Instagram to promote your business, use professional-quality photographs.

Virtual events. Networking changed during the worst part of the global COVID-19 pandemic. Online events and work, as well as networking, increased. This shows little sign of abating. If you attend a virtual networking event, keep it professional—make it known you have a business background; offer input but don't hog the event; ensure your messaging is clear.

What's your elevator pitch? An elevator pitch is a thirty-second sound bite of who you are and what you are about. "My name is _____. I am president of XYZ Company. I rehab and transform houses."

Local Government

You might think that in your house-flipping business you need to know developers, real estate brokers, contractors, and the various people we discuss in **T: Team.** But you will also need to network and know your city council members, mayor, and the city manager where you live, *especially* if you intend to go into commercial real estate development eventually or scale your business.

So, for example, if you have land you intend to develop—your project will need approval. In certain areas, that is not a simple proposition. In fact, there are places where the process is painful. Getting to know the players in decision-making for places in which you wish to flip houses and do any kind of development is something you will find valuable at some point.

Who Do You Need in Your Network?

We discuss real estate brokers in **B: Brokers** and others in **T: Team,** but briefly, here are some of the types of people you should be trying to get in your network.

- Brokers
- Real estate attorneys (both buy side and sell side)
- Architects
- Certified public accountants
- Wholesalers
- Contractors
- Subcontractors

- Plumbers
- Electricians
- Stagers
- Title companies
- Carpenters
- Window installers
- Garage door installers
- Flooring installers
- Roofers
- Pool repairers
- Drywallers
- Cabinet installers
- Landscapers
- Property managers
- Land surveyors
- Lenders (both banks and hard money lenders, as well as investors and investment groups)
- Insurance companies
- Interior designers (especially if you are going to do commercial investment eventually)
- House cleaning crews
- Junk haulers
- Real estate appraisers

Offers and Contracts

Let's start with the obvious. You need a real estate attorney. This is especially important when you are starting out as a house flipper, because you may not know some of the fine print and clauses that are important. However, this entry will look at the general things to pay attention to.

Contingencies

A contingency clause (and there are different types) is sort of like "an offer … but …" The contract is not legally binding until that "but" is met. Some contingencies are as follows:

- Financing contingency: This means the buyer is not held to the offer unless their mortgage or financing goes through. In a hot market, this kind of contingency likely won't occur because most people trying to buy a home in that kind of market condition know they need to come with a cash offer or with a preapproved mortgage in hand. However, it can happen. There are usually time constraints as well, so you know whether the bid is actually going to go through.

- Home inspection contingency: This contingency allows the buyer to have a home inspection company come to inspect the house (usually it will be within a set amount of time, preferably pretty quickly if a problem does crop up that needs to be repaired or fixed prior to closing). If the inspection turns up something major (like foundation issues), the buyer can back out of the contract (usually, again, within a specific time frame, often seven days). If there are a number of small things (which can add up to a lot), there can be negotiation between the seller and the buyer (or, often, their real estate agents) on what will be fixed—or financial concessions to the buyer.

- Appraisal contingency: If a buyer makes an offer based on how much their mortgage is approved for, the value of the house must be equal to or more than that number. So, for example, if a buyer puts down $60,000 on a $300,000 house, the mortgage company is loaning the buyer $240,000. If the house only appraises at $230,000, there is a problem and the mortgage may not be granted at that price.

- Home sale contingency: In a cold market, where buyers have more of the power, a seller might accept an offer with this. In a hot market, you definitely wouldn't. These are contingencies that tend to be problematic. What the offer is stating is that the buyer will purchase the house *if or when* the sale of their existing home goes through. Perhaps they have an offer and intend to close on their existing home in thirty days. However, if you have started house flipping or read and studied enough about real estate transactions, you know anything could go wrong in this scenario. What if their home doesn't pass inspection? Or their buyer's financing falls through? Like a procession of dominoes, things can fall, one after the other, until your deal derails.

Contingencies (and addenda) add potential problems to a home purchase. If you are the seller, you will want your lawyer to look at them carefully.

Earnest Money

Earnest money tells you a buyer is earnest and sincere about wanting to buy a particular house. They provide a check for, usually, 1 or 2 percent of the agreed-on home price. So, for a $300,000 house, that might be $3,000 to $6,000. In a hot market, people might compete on bids for a house and offer more earnest money. This money is placed in escrow. When the deal goes through, the money is released and put toward the down payment on the house.

Earnest money also has a window—let's say a week. If the buyer gets a home inspection in that time, for example, and a major issue comes up, the buyer can back out and receive their earnest money back.

On the flip side, I know of an older woman, a retired college professor, who put down earnest money of $15,000 on an older home that needed some work in a trendy part of her city. But as time went on, she realized it was too big an undertaking. She walked away—and the seller kept her earnest money (fortunately, she was in a position to do so financially—and she went on to get a beautiful loft condo with zero upkeep and no need of fixing up).

Parts of the Contract

Real estate contracts will be a little different depending on what state you are in. But in general, these are the elements of a contract:

- Who's the buyer? Who is the seller?

- Address, survey description.

- Sale price.

- How much (if any) earnest money is the buyer putting up?

- How will the buyer be paying the balance of the cost of the house? Deposit (and how much)?

- Closing date.

- All cash? Financing? If financing, what are the details? Is the seller responsible for any of the elements?

- Contingencies, if any.

- Any liens on the property? Who is discharging them?

- Any warranties?

- Conveyances? (For example, if the buyer pays for some of the furnishings or elements like chandeliers, lighting, certain appliances—again, this varies by state.)

- Who is insuring the property prior to closing?

- Recording fees?

- Who is paying for the survey?

- Who is responsible for title and title insurance?

- Broker's fees.

- Special provisions?

- Closing costs?

- Can closing costs or other elements above and beyond the house sale price be folded into the mortgage?

Closing Costs

When you purchase a house, the purchase price is not going to be the total price or amount of money you will need or finance. Closing costs are, essentially, processing (and inspection and other) fees you pay for buying the house. Often the seller will pay for all or some of them—but in a hot market, the buyer may pay all or most of them.

Closing costs can be as much as 5 or 6 percent of the cost of the house. So, especially if you are just starting out, be sure your financing will cover this. These closing costs can include the following:

- **Appraisal.** This is something (especially) that your financing company or lender will want. It ensures the house is worth the price you are paying for it. This could cost a few hundred dollars.

- **Application fee.** If you are not doing a cash offer, this is the cost for filing a loan application. Again, it will vary by state and lender, but it will be a few hundred dollars, usually.

- **Attorney fees.** Most closings are done at an attorney's office (well, since the COVID-19 pandemic, things are more virtual these days). The real estate attorney is the one who handles the closing. They will have all the paperwork already drawn up—and will point out *all* the places you have to initial and sign on all the various copies at closing!

- **Closing fee.** This is the cost of the closing itself—also usually paid to a real estate attorney.

- **Credit report fee.** If a buyer is financing the purchase of a property instead of doing all cash, the buyer will pay for the cost of getting their credit report done so that the lender can make sure their credit is good enough to do the loan.

- **Courier fee.** Papers are often transferred between the parties of a real estate transaction—you may have to pay for that.

- **Discount points.** Again, if financing, this is a fee a buyer can pay to reduce the amount of money they have to put down for a deposit. It isn't mandatory and is only paid for if the buyer qualifies and needs to do so. Note, the next entry is the mortgage insurance fee. A buyer will likely have to pay for private mortgage insurance (PMI) if they use discount points.

- **Mortgage insurance fee.** Again, depending on how a buyer is financing a house, the lender may require them to pay a fee that insures the mortgage. In cases where a buyer puts down a deposit of less than 20 percent of the purchase price (sometimes through discount points, sometimes for special mortgages in certain states for teachers or public sector workers), they will be required in most places to get PMI (which you will often see on contracts).

- **Homeowner association (HOA) fees.** If the house is part of a homeowner association, fees will be paid up front to transfer the ownership to the new buyer.

- **Land survey fees.** This is a fee paid for a survey to be done.

- **Homeowner's insurance.** A house will have to be insured—so the buyer will pay for this at closing.

- **Title insurance.** Yet another fee (they all add up). This one can cost half a percentage point of the purchase price or 1 percent (it varies by state). Owner's title insurance means if five years down the road a lien is discovered, the insurance will pay for it (but you will want a title search done if you are the buyer to try to make sure this is not an issue).

- **Pest inspection, lead paint inspection.** The buyer may have to pay for a pest inspection (certain states require it, especially to ensure there is no termite damage). If the home was built prior to 1979, the buyer will need a lead paint inspection too.

- **Property taxes.** You may (as a buyer) be required to pay for a year of property taxes up front at closing. The cost obviously depends on what the home costs.

- **Local taxes.** Some places charge a tax to transfer the title of a property from one buyer to another.

- **Underwriter fee.** If the buyer is using a mortgage and not all cash, the lender will likely require them to pay for the lender verifying the information on the mortgage application. This can be hundreds of dollars.

Depending on where you live and what type of loan the buyer is using, there can be other fees. An+ FHA loan will have fees. A VA loan (for veterans for buying a home) will have fees. In addition, sometimes closing costs (or some of them) will be paid for by the buyer (in cold markets). Sometimes the buyer will be able to finance some of these fees by adding them into the total mortgage.

Seller's Disclosure

If a house is not brand new—in other words, if the buyer is buying it from the previous occupant—the seller is required by law to provide a seller's disclosure form. This form requires the seller to reveal problems with the house. It needs to be *fully* filled out. Seller's disclosures must reveal certain specific issues:

- **Deaths in the home related to home issues or violent crime.** Not every state requires disclosures about deaths (particularly natural causes or illness-related deaths). However, if, for example, someone fell from a balcony on the home where the wood was rotted and the person consequently died, then it would need to be disclosed. If the home had a murder occur in it, then most states require that disclosure.

- **Hazards or contamination.** In California (a state where earthquakes occur), for example, a seller would have to tell a new buyer if the home is situated on a fault line. In a place with flood plains, that natural disaster risk must be disclosed. If radon or other toxicities were once in the home, most states require that be disclosed. In short, if there's hazardous waste or the site of natural disasters, you usually have to tell the seller.

- **Neighborhood nuisance issues.** We tend to think of neighborhood nuisances as something like a terrible neighbor who routinely hosts very loud parties all night long (playing EDM music with a bass line that is so loud your bed shakes). However, in real estate terms on the seller's disclosure, it actually generally means things like a military base where explosions or gunfire can be audibly heard in the yard of the house (a friend of mine has a house where military helicopters fly over several times each day and night—and they are *not* quiet). If there is a fertilizer factory or a landfill or other odorous issues nearby, that must be disclosed. If a factory spews smoke in the air, affecting visibility in the neighborhood, that would be another nuisance.

- **Homeowner association information.** This includes the rules of the association. Some are truly onerous and overbearing. This also includes the cost of fines for infractions, the cost of dues, and impending assessments. For example, in areas of Florida, communities, condo owners, and residents may be required to pay a portion of the cost for dredging sand to maintain beaches. A large condo association may need upcoming roof or HVAC work, assessing each owner thousands of dollars. In addition, the buyer can (and should) ask for information on the homeowner association financials. You may recall the horrific Surfside condominium collapse in South Florida. Nearly one hundred people died, and hundreds more were displaced and lost their homes and belongings. In the aftermath, it came to light that engineering repairs were needed, but the condo association had been putting them off due to the financial issues of the association and the high cost.

- **Repair history.** Some states require that the seller reveal major repairs. This includes roof repairs, foundation repairs, defects in the floors—essentially major things that may affect the home's value and structural integrity.

- **Water damage.** If, every time it rains, water pools in a crawlspace or in a basement (or the roof leaks), this must be disclosed.

- **What comes with the house?** This is important to the buyer. If a buyer tours a home and is enamored of its beautiful chandelier in the foyer or window treatments and blinds, they will want to look for what is conveyed in the seller's disclosure or negotiate to buy those items.

Profits

No one should be reading this book and thinking, "How can I do everything the cheapest to maximize my profits?" The fact is profits are a fine line between going overboard with luxury items you will not recoup in the sales price and going so inexpensive that your homes do not stand the test of time and look shoddy, poorly done, or simply ugly.

We'll (yet again) repeat the 70 Percent Rule:

THE 70 PERCENT RULE

Most home flippers use the 70 Percent Rule to determine whether to purchase a home. This is the estimated value of the house after repairs are made as well as the estimated repair costs using this simple formula:

After-repair value (ARV) × 0.70 – Estimated repair costs = Maximum buying price

Ideally you want to maximize profits without sacrificing quality.

Time Is Money

When it comes to profits, there is probably no greater challenge than *time*. The more time a house takes to get to a showable level, the less profit you will make.

The clock is ticking the moment you contract for a house. Your team needs to be assembled *before* the ink is dry. But in addition, you will want to organize the steps in your renovation so that the rehab makes orderly sense. This can be difficult when you are just starting out and don't have a lot of experience with how things go. The last thing you want is to have subcontractors come to work on the house when you are not quite ready for them or you have not bundled the projects so they can get it all done in a set time or if you have to send them to another house and call them back later.

> **When it comes to profits, there is probably no greater challenge than *time*.**

This is the rough order of how to flip a house for the best profit/time management.

1. Have all permits and surveys ready. Do major structural repairs (keeping in mind you want to try to avoid these) first, such as foundations. Handle any mold problems or plumbing/water retention issues. Go ahead and get started on external elements, such as tree removal, hauling off dead branches, and filling in or fixing a pool.

2. Next, schedule roof and gutter repairs or the installation of new ones. This is the time to put in new windows. If replacing siding, schedule that.

3. Inside: Demo (short for demolition)—this is the time to knock down walls or rip out cabinets. Begin to rough in wiring or plumbing (if inspections are needed, schedule those so that does not hold you up—you want the inspection *before* you put walls back up); handle any HVAC or thermostat issues; install a new water heater if needed.

4. Fix subfloors (after taking up old flooring if needed). You will want to replace any subfloor badly damaged by water, for example. You'll also try to fix them if they are uneven.

5. If you are creating a walk-in closet; putting up a half wall, breakfast bar, or wall; expanding a room; or creating two rooms out of one big one, frame that in.

6. If adding or redoing a deck, have that going on simultaneously. (An outdoor space is increasingly something buyers want.)

7. Inside: Add insulation (including in attic to make the home more energy-efficient); do drywall/sheetrock work.

8. Replace any interior doors as needed.

9. Interior painting and trim work.

10. Install new cabinets or vanities, new countertops, new knobs.

11. Any wiring or plumbing finishes.

12. New flooring.

13. New tiles in bathroom/other rooms; backsplashes.

14. Install new appliances.

15. Landscaping. Curb appeal.

16. Punch list.

17. Final inspections.

18. Staging.

19. Sell it!

20. Walk-through for buyer.

Punch List

A punch list is essentially a to-do list. You will have two as you flip houses. The first is for *you*. It is the punch list you make as the house progresses so you can tick things off as you visit the site and see what your contractors and subcontractors have done. This also helps you communicate with them about the timeline and what they still need to get done.

The second punch list will be when there is a final walk-through for the buyer. If you are meticulous in your own punch list, ideally nothing will come up.

When it gets down to the end, to those final punch lists, just know sometimes the little things will be a pain in the neck. I remember one house I flipped where, unbeknownst to me, there was some sort of wiring issue with a single recessed bathroom light. I replaced the lightbulb three times—it kept shorting out when people toured the house. We fixed it, but it was one of those things that doesn't cost a lot of money but just needs to be taken care of.

(🏠) FLIP TIP

Make sure you have your team assembled before the ink is even dry on the contract of a house you buy. The minute you take possession of the house, you should have your team there—knocking down walls, starting on the roof, or taking out windows. Every single solitary day counts.

Things That Can Eat Your Profits

There are elements of house flipping that will cut into your profits. Certain repairs, certain roadblocks, can take you from profitable to just making a minimal profit (leaving you less capital to move on to your next flip).

Here are some of the pitfalls:

- **Pools.** I've discussed elsewhere that pools are rarely worth the investment. The exception is a high-end flip where a spa or hot tub might be a wow factor for the backyard or if you are in a part of the country/neighborhood where it's almost expected. That said, even if that is the case, if you are buying a distressed home that has been neglected, pools are big-ticket items to fix—tiles, plumbing, hidden leaks. I've filled in more than one pool in the course of my career.

- **Expensive flooring.** Again, with the exception of a luxury flip, expensive flooring may not make sense. There are too many great products out there, like luxury vinyl flooring (LVT), that look great but won't blow your budget. LVT is very durable, and the plethora of choices make it a great choice that looks good and is also easy for the new owners to take care of.

In family neighborhoods where it's more likely you will be selling to people with children (and often pets), this is a type of flooring that is especially appreciated.

- **Foundation problems.** These are never easy to solve. Always be on the lookout for cracks in foundations.

- **Water damage.** This can be behind walls, or you may become aware of standing water after storms in basements, for example.

- **Termite infestation or damage.**

- **Plumbing or wiring issues.** With both of these, if you decide to purchase a house and you discover these issues, you will want to be sure you do the repairs *first* in your projects lineup and then worry about flooring, painting walls, etc. Both of these issues are often behind walls—so you want them resolved first.

- **Adding bathrooms or bedrooms.** Sometimes smaller, older homes will have only one bath (I know, I don't know how they managed, either, especially with kids). Or it's only two bedrooms, and the location in a family-friendly neighborhood suggests most buyers will want a third. These are major renovations, and you should think carefully about this (most especially, you do not want to take on a flip with major structural changes as your first flip).

Lower-Cost Fixes for Your Fixer-Upper

Not everything costs a lot of money when working on your flip. Here are some lower-cost fixes.

- **Curb appeal:** Clear old leaves and dead shrubs; trim back shrubs or trees. Install a new mailbox. Paint the front door. Power wash (you would be surprised how a good power wash can make the house look cleaner—but make sure you do the walkways and driveway. It makes such a difference). New mulch. When ready to show the house, be sure the lawn is freshly mowed.

- **Inside (everywhere):** Clean everything spotless. Spackle nail holes and imperfections on the walls. Fresh paint everywhere. Make sure all the windows are clean (and the screens and the sills too!). Replace old registers with new brass ones or new neutral ones.

- **Kitchen and bathrooms:** New sinks, new vanities, new lights/fixtures (it goes without saying that all lightbulbs everywhere in the house should be new and working). Scrub the inside of cabinets and drawers. If needed, put new contact paper down. Scrub or bleach the grout. Fresh caulking in the shower or bathtub. New backsplash in the kitchen (adds a great wow for not a lot of cost).

- **Putting a bathtub in the primary bathroom, if there isn't one.** People definitely ask about and want a tub, especially in the primary bathroom. Parents of young kids want them, too, to make bathing babies and toddlers easier.

- **Not entirely low-cost, but necessary:** replace old/worn carpeting; update flooring; add new windows if the old ones do not bring in enough light.

(🏠) FLIP TIP

The off-season is a great time to negotiate with contractors and others who want to stay busy. You have a little extra bargaining leverage.

Renovations That Don't Add Value to Your Flip

Some renovations simply do not add value to the house, or they cost more than they are worth. These include the following:

- **Pools.** I must sound like I hate pools! But they are often a hidden money pit. Remember, most house flipping means distressed properties. Therefore, they are even more likely to have issues.

- **Expensive bathroom remodels (especially if the neighborhood is more modest).** New vanities, new paint, and new fixtures don't have to cost too much. Most people are looking for double sinks in the primary bathroom especially, so adding that doesn't break the bank and is worth it. However, adding expensive features like jacuzzi tubs or complicated and expensive tile patterns on the floors or shower walls, for example, don't usually recoup your cost (again, especially in more modest neighborhoods).

- **Home theaters.** Some people might like one, but it truly is not recouped because it's not something people feel they must have. It tends to be a less-used room, as most families these days all have televisions and electronics in the bedrooms. I think they are wasted space for a flip.

- **Luxury kitchen remodels.** The rule you must follow is remembering that this is a flip—it is not your own home. While you might like a Viking range or high-end marble, unless this is a luxury flip, the places to spend money are nice, solid cabinets, new stainless appliances, new flooring, and adding a backsplash and new fixtures. *Great looking* doesn't have to mean *expensive* these days.

- **High-end landscaping.** You definitely need curb appeal, but a house flip is not the place to put in trees costing hundreds of dollars each.

So How Much Profit Can You Make?

The 70 Percent Rule appears several times in this book because it's one of the primary calculations all house flippers use. It means, in plain English, that you should not pay more for a property than 70 percent of a house's ARV *less the costs of the renovation.*

While this is a simple formula used by everyone in the house-flipping business, it is actually *not* that simple. That phrase, "less the costs of the renovation," means you need to be pretty accurate as far as the costs of the renovations before you even close on the property. This is pretty easy for me now—I know what permits and plumbers and electricians and hauling companies all cost—in other words, all the moving parts of a renovation. But when I was starting, I definitely made mistakes that cost me money.

In normal market conditions, house flippers typically average about $25,000 to $30,000 profit per flip. The people who have a system and teams in place tend to do better. In a hot market, that profit can leap up—sometimes near $100,000 in some places. In a cold market, flippers might not make the $30,000 average. For example, in a hot market, you may have multiple bids and houses sell in under a week. You may not even have to stage the house (which obviously costs money). In a slower market, you may have to pay utilities, insurance, staging costs, and more for *months* until the house sells. Therefore, you will want to always be on top of what is happening in the market where you live or flip.

Expect the Unexpected

When I was flipping, I knew I could absorb the unexpected in a house flip. So if a pipe burst, or the house needed a new HVAC unit that I didn't plan on, I still made a profit and was not too stressed out. However, if you are doing your first flip, you need to be aware that many things can go awry.

As I've said elsewhere, do not be lulled by beautiful homes on design and flipping shows. Even when they show "disasters" where things go wrong, the hosts always finish on time, and the results are always spectacular. Thus, it is very important that you always have a cushion in your renovation budget. One of the dangers of being new to flipping is not having enough money to complete the project in a timely fashion—if something derails your timeline or budget, you need to be prepared. (We'll talk about this in letter *X*.)

FLIP TIP

Make sure your budget—and timeline—can adapt for bad weather. If you schedule your exterior painting or major land-scaping project and then the entire week is pouring rain, you need to pivot and adapt so you don't lose time and money. Be ready to do interior projects and get ahead inside.

Protect Your Investment

A friend of mine was rehabbing a house while she was living in it. She and her boyfriend took a vacation, and when she returned, all the copper piping on the house had been stolen. Another friend's parents bought a house and completed the remodel—all that was left to do were some punch items and installing the new refrigerator. This was a high-end project (a 5,200-square-foot home). Five days before closing, vandals broke in, drank beer in the basement, leaving a mess—and intentionally set a fire. The entire house filled with smoke, though thank goodness there was no structural damage, thanks to an observant neighbor who called the police.

To ensure your maximum profit and to protect your investment, use some commonsense approaches.

However, the house had to be completely cleaned by professionals and all new paint done, in addition to needing to replace carpeting in the primary bedroom.

You need to be sure your job site is safe and protected as much as possible from theft, vandalism, or other problems. Thieves might even be from a work crew—there are just so many people going into your rehab house and on your job site. Therefore, to ensure your maximum profit and to protect your investment, use some commonsense approaches:

- Ensure doors and windows are all locked (solid/new locks on the exterior doors are essential; you might put a new steel door for the front).

- Consider having security cameras (new products like the Ring doorbell are low-cost ways to keep an eye out). I know a house flipper who doesn't put in security—but has signs that say he does in prominent spots in the landscaping and near the front door.

- Ensure tools are locked up or not left on the job site. Ask your contractors to take their expensive tools home at night.

- If you have tile or other materials delivered to the site, keep them in a locked garage until you use them.

- Exterior lights need to be one of the first things you install. A dark, empty house is just too much of a temptation.

- Meet the neighbors! As I shared in my story where an observant neighbor prevented even greater damage from vandals, it's beneficial to be friendly with the neighbors near your property. First, you are getting your name and brand out there—these people could be good referrals or may spread the word a house is coming up for sale. Second, they may keep an eye on your site, as they don't want thieves or trouble in their neighborhood either.

QuickBooks and Accounting

Setting up your business the right way from the start is much easier than trying to retroactively accomplish things down the road. As you saw in **E: Entity**, there are different approaches to setting up a house-flipping and renovation business. Some people, for whom it's a side hustle, may opt to do it in their own name and try to keep it simple. Others, like myself, set up a corporate entity, identity, and branding from the start. Having this brand has allowed me, as my career as a flipper has grown, to branch off into other business investing, which is now the focus on my company.

Regardless of your setup, what is most important is tracking your expenses—and paying your bills. And doing so professionally! Having an accountant is wonderful (and important come tax time). But like many small businesses—especially if you are just starting—

the tracking of expenses will be done in QuickBooks or some other accounting software program.

Accounting Software, Including QuickBooks

One of the advantages of QuickBooks is that not only are you running your operations like a business, but it is already designed to handle just about any aspect of the accounting side of business.

We all know stories of people who show up to their accountants' office or their bookkeepers' office with plastic bags filled with receipts and no order or organization to it. QuickBooks avoids that nightmare—as long as you use it properly.

QuickBooks is owned by Intuit. There are other software programs around. According to *Business News Daily*, the top-five alternative software programs are Xero, Sage, Zoho, Wave (which is free), and FreshBooks.[21] However, you will want to be sure whatever program you use can communicate with your bank, set up sales tax, etc.

Some QuickBooks features include the following:

- Tracking income, including payments from vendors

- Tracking expenses

- Invoicing

- Estimating

- Working with business bank accounts

- Managing sales tax

- Payroll

- Cash flow planning and reports

- Mileage tracking

- Receipt capturing (now, so many programs have it so you can simply take a photo and then categorize it)

- Direct deposit

- 1099s

- Tracking 401(k)s and other human resources functions

What if you've never worked with a program like this before? The good news is that if you are on LinkedIn, you may be aware the company acquired Lynda for $1.5 billion.[22] It is now called LinkedIn Learning and offers a broad variety of classes.

LinkedIn Learning offers specific QuickBooks courses. However, they also offer courses on bookkeeping and other aspects of accounts payables and receivables and pretty much anything else you might want to learn about taking care of your company books—whether that person is you or someone you hire.

Spreadsheets

Just the word *spreadsheets* can make some people break out in hives. This might be you too! I know very few people who love Excel. Again, LinkedIn provides training classes and courses on its use plus mini-courses for quick tips and hints.

I recommend spreadsheets on every individual project so you can compare them against each project's status and spending. This isn't something to just access for tax time in April, or even once a quarter. You will want to stay on top of these spreadsheets a minimum of twice a month—and sometimes more.

The complexity of what you track will vary as you grow. It also depends on what hats you wear. Some people, as I've pointed out, go into house flipping because they have the actual construction skills to do some or most of the work on a house. Others oversee the operations. Excel is noted for working with the construction industry, where it can track workflow and estimating, not just profits and losses.

Maybe It's Time for an Accountant

Success creates new problems for small business owners. They are good problems to have (usually), but at some point, most small companies experience growing pains.

If you are tracking one house project's expenditures, you still need to be vigilant about tracking all your incoming money as well as outgoing expenses, mileage, etc. But it's doable—for one house. Or two. But at some point, when you have multiple houses, it will be clear that tracking all this is nearly a full-time job (or certainly a very intense part-time job). Remember that every house will be at a different stage—one might just be starting; another might be at punch-list time.

At some point, most small companies experience growing pains.

We have always had an accountant—especially as we've grown (and now we are doing investments—there is even more to keep track of). However, I still like to keep my hand in it—I like being aware of what's going on with our financials.

Anticipate Financial Growth

Remember how I said that it is so much easier to have your business entity set up from the start? The same will go for your banking.

It is a good idea to have a relationship with a banker or lender. You also want to have your banking (especially if incorporating and planning on expansion over time) with a financial institution you think will be able to serve your needs as you grow larger, such as getting into commercial development. If you think catching up on tracking receipts is a pain in the neck, think about switching banks once you have several projects in the pipeline.

A bank can offer credit lines, letters for potential investors, as well as investment accounts and the day-in and day-out banking of your business.

In Favor of Credit Cards

As of this writing, changes are underway in how the IRS approaches cash apps like Venmo. Today, there are as many ways to pay people as there are apps. However, there are disadvantages to paying people through Venmo, not the least of which is tracking it. These days, many people with side hustles, as well as companies that do landscaping or cleaning services, for example, may use Venmo or another cash app. It's easy for them to collect money from clients while they are out and about, as well as use it for cash flow.

However, you will want to track your expenses—and this is why I like paying with a corporate credit card. It works hand in glove with our accounting programs. This keeps our work-related expenditures together. We get a monthly statement. It's just a terrific way to track our outflow of money. (Not to mention, many cards have rewards programs, cash back on expenses, or other perks.)

Don't Forget the Unique Expenses of House Flipping

If you are getting started as a house flipper, there is definitely a learning curve. There will be expenditures you have not counted on, for example, as well as costs unique to this business.

A good example is home insurance. For most home buyers, your home insurance is rolled into your monthly payment, and it is renewed year to year. In the case of house flipping, you need to work with an insurer who will do the insurance month to month (since as soon as your sale closes, you are canceling the insurance).

Appraisals are another expense that increases as you expand your real estate portfolio.

HOUSE FLIPPING EXPENSES FOR TAX PURPOSES

The following is by no means a complete list. But here are some common house-flipping expenses to track for tax-write-off purposes. Again, every company is different; every house flipper is different— you need to consult your own tax accountant about what pertains to you, both for federal taxes and taxes in your home state.

- The cost of the house itself

- All materials used on the project—roof tiles, flooring, cabinets, rugs, windows, etc.

- Labor related to the project—all your subcontractors, from the landscapers you use to roofers, plus people on your payroll

- Cost of running your office, whether that is a home office or in a rented office space elsewhere

- Utilities—electric, gas, water

- Depreciation of equipment you own

- Advertising

- Marketing costs

- Insurance

- Real estate taxes related to the property

Capital Gains

Capital gains is one of the trickier aspects to tax liability. Obviously, if you are flipping houses, you want to avoid a capital gains tax. Avoiding that will depend on how you financed your house flip.

Capital gains, in a nutshell, is the difference in a price paid versus what it sold for, adjusting for commissions and fees paid during the transaction. Income level and how long you held onto a property (this usually applies to family homes held for years) affect at what percent capital gains are charged. In the house-flipping business, it will also depend on whether your business is your full-time employment or your side hustle.

Rentals

The COVID-19 pandemic's effect on the housing market, inflation, interest rates, relocations, hot areas, and many other factors all influence whether a house flipper should consider entering the rental market or sell off the property instead. Assuming you want to do rentals, here are some considerations.

What Kind of Rentals?

Once upon a real estate time, rentals were apartments, condos, or houses, usually rented year to year. No more. Today we have short-term rentals, long-term rentals, executive rentals (which usually come furnished), Airbnbs, Vrbo, and more.

LONG-TERM RENTALS

Location is everything when it comes to all kinds of rentals, but in terms of long-term rentals, it's a different kind of location from short-term and vacation rentals. When it's a long-term rental, you want to be close to a big company's headquarters or in the neighborhoods that are near schools, etc.

In general, in the long-term market, for profitable rentals you generally are trying to appeal to people with kids or executives and employees of large corporations.

Many people believe rentals are a great way to make money. In fact, it is most often called *passive income*. But actually, it's very much *active.* If you are starting out and do not have the money or profit margin yet to hire a management company, then you are the point of contact for your renter. From an air conditioner that conks out to leaky faucets or roofs, you will need to make repairs or hire someone to. Be sure you have allotted for this both in terms of time and money.

This is also the case of the "Goldilocks" house. You don't want something too huge in a long-term rental (there are few families that need a six-bedroom house, for example). Nor do you want something too small that cannot at least accommodate one or two kids. So you are in the area of "just right" houses, which are usually between 1,800 and 2,000 square feet, fairly standard homes, ideally in a safe neighborhood that is well maintained.

If you are renting the house out yourself, not through a management company (who, if reliable, will conduct background and credit checks on renters), you will want to be very careful of whom you rent to. You will want to ensure they are employed, and check their credit score. Check references. And remember, renting out a house is a risk too. I know someone who rented her property and did due diligence on her renter. A police officer with a wife who was a teacher and two kids, with good credit. But the police officer and his wife split up in what became an ugly divorce. She left him completely—and they needed both incomes to afford the house. He was distraught and defaulted—and then this real estate property owner needed to go through the steps of eviction. So, again, expect the unexpected.

Considering that the latest survey of American pet ownership indicates 70 percent of American households have either a dog or cat,[23] it can be difficult if you exclude those with pets from long-term rentals. However, it is logical to ask for a pet deposit. In addition, you should assume if someone has a dog or cat—or a few kids—you are going to be cleaning or replacing the carpet at the end of the rental before you get another tenant.

Short-Term and Vacation Rentals

Location, location, location. Only this time, it's for other reasons.

When it comes to houses used as Airbnbs, the location is even more critical. Short-term rentals in residential areas aren't as needed. But rentals in exciting cities like Austin, Nashville, Seattle, and Miami, for example, are needed as people gather and want to be part of the nightlife and energy those places those cities offer.

According to Hostaway.com, these are the best *urban* areas in which to invest in an Airbnb:[24]

- San Francisco, California

- Denver, Colorado

- Los Angeles, California

- New York, New York

- Portland, Oregon

- Boston, Massachusetts

- Dallas, Texas

- Honolulu, Hawaii

- Phoenix, Arizona

In terms of vacation areas to invest in Airbnbs, it's no surprise that the beach takes the lead. Hawaii, the beaches of North Carolina, Florida, and Tennessee lake beach areas, and other shore cities in warmer climates are the most popular, along with Anaheim, California (near Disneyland), as well as cities known for their nightlife, like Nashville and New Orleans.[25]

For short-term rentals, consider your location and do some research. In a city or near a city, you are more likely to have business travelers or couples, and condos make sense. In a beach community, families often vacation together, and you need a home that can accommodate them. In some high-end beach communities, you will find investors who purchase five- and six-bedroom (or more!) homes, furnish them in beach chic, and rent them for family reunions and summer vacationers.

Wherever you are considering investing in your short-term rental, make sure you do your due diligence and research whether there are limitations on short-term rentals. Some cities have been restricting Airbnbs through regulations. One reason is tightening housing markets; Airbnbs can cut into affordable housing. Other reasons include noise and partying in residential locations or places like New York City where many if not most apartment complexes, condos, and co-ops have rules regarding short-term rentals.

Management Companies

If you decide to enter into the short-term rental/vacation rental market, you will need to decide who is managing your property.

First, maybe you think that person is you. Consider why you entered into the house-flipping business. Was it to be a property superintendent and make arrangements and do repairs? Or was it to … flip properties?

Second, if you invest in a city that is not where you live, you will have a harder time managing your vacation property than if you live nearby. You can't evaluate the work of repair people, for example, the same as if you live in town and can take a look.

Short or long term, many people contract with a management company. Some specialize in short-term markets, and others may focus on yearly rentals.

This is by no means a complete list, but management companies typically take care of these aspects:

- Screen applicants, do the background checks, collect deposits, etc.

- Arrange for and coordinate maintenance

- Market your property

- Handle the legal aspects

- Handle the financial aspects

- Communicate with your tenants about issues

When choosing a management company, consider the following:

- Look for a company that fits your type of rental. Is it a company that deals with vacation homes and condos all the time? Is it a company that handles whole apartment complexes? Do they mostly do residential homes in the neighborhoods where you are investing? For example, in beach communities, there are certain kinds of maintenance that need to be done—air conditioners and anything outside that gets more wear and tear from salty air and sand. Those beach rentals could be in an area that regularly gets hit with hurricanes, which requires its own kind of preparation. Beach rentals in popular party areas also require a management company that can crack down on house parties and ensure that thirty wild college kids are not all sleeping in a four-bedroom house.

- It goes without saying that any management company you hire should have the right licenses, insurance, etc.

- Get referrals and check references (one reason **N: Networking** is so important).

- Make sure you understand the property management agreement—especially your first one. If you have a lawyer, it would be a good idea to have him or her look it over.

Decor and Finishes on Your Rental

If you have ever lived at the beach or rented there every summer, you know what kind of a beating vacation homes, especially rentals, can take. First, you have the elements. Winds, hurricanes and tropical storms, heavy rains, beating sun.

Next, no matter how hard everyone tries—sand gets dragged in the house, wet bathing suits get dropped on the bathroom floors, wet towels accumulate in bedroom corners. On vacation, many people are a bit more carefree about how they handle laundry or tidiness—it's vacation, after all!

The key to owning a short-term rental is easy-to-maintain furnishings and decor. You are going to be cycling through renters weekly. You are bound to lose items here and there—someone accidentally takes something home (or on purpose!), or it gets lost at the beach. Those wet bathing suits, sand, people eating on couches, partiers spilling drinks. A rowdy event where someone breaks something.

The key to owning a short-term rental is easy-to-maintain furnishings and decor.

On the flip side, in order to compete it must be neat, tidy, and elegant. The highest-rated Airbnbs have a certain vibe—boho chic, modern, "Coastal Grandmother," etc. You need TVs, some decor. Artwork, framed pictures on the wall, a vase here, a coffee table with a jar of shells there.

Furniture should be easy to clean—and easy to move. Remember, in between each renter, a cleaning crew will be trying to quickly turn the house over for the next renter the same day as checkout. However, I would not recommend the cheapest furniture out there—because it simply will not hold up. Not to mention, cheaply made chairs, couches, and tables sometimes have issues—like springs that pinch in a pullout couch—or they are not sturdy. You don't need a guest to pinch a finger or use a lightweight table that collapses.

Make sure there is enough lighting. For today's traveler, Wi-Fi and a workspace are also essential. The era of remote work means vacations have changed—and some people are full-time digital nomads.

Think of extras that people appreciate (and leave positive comments about on reviews): high chairs; baby gates (good safety consideration if there are stairs in your rental); beach toys; a stroller; coffee machine (essential) and coffee (nice gesture); kitchen basics like tin foil, plastic baggies, salt and pepper; board games; hair dryer; Tupperware containers; pots big enough for large family dinners at a family vacation rental (nothing worse than traveling with eight people, wanting to make a pot of spaghetti, and only finding a two-quart pot); extra blankets, along with blanket throws for the couch so people can cuddle with them while they watch TV.

Another thing that is essential is frequent checking that items are in good shape. It's very disconcerting to a vacationer to check into a home and pull out pots that look like they were acquired in a garage sale in 1972.

Consider that you will have to repaint a short-term rental more often. You don't want to necessarily choose the most expensive paint. Or, for that matter, carpet or finishes. For something like the kitchen, if you go with granite, choose a darker color. If you choose cabinetry, choose something that will hide scratches well. Think with sturdiness and attractiveness—together—in mind.

Tiny Homes

I would be remiss if I did not include tiny homes in our "Rentals" chapter. Once upon a time, people wanted houses to be big, big, big. Now, television shows, communities, and people all over are thinking tiny, tiny, tiny.

Tiny homes are generally designed to be clever. If space is at a premium, then every inch of a tiny home has to work to conserve it. Features like hidden storage and bookshelves or using nooks in unique ways are a hallmark of tiny homes.

Tiny homes can be a good way to enter the rental market. For one thing, they are popular right now. They also cost less, so there is a lower barrier to entry in the Airbnb market for a tiny home. They are easy to clean and care for, and since you will likely be renting to single people or couples, less wear and tear.

One more point about tiny homes as rentals—it's still location, location, location. Tiny homes are often situated on land. Because of this, make sure you use the *outside* space of your rental well, whether that is a fire pit and bistro lights, with comfortable Adirondack chairs, a deck, or other ways to make the outdoors part of your offering.

One Last Thing: Photography

One last tip for short-term and vacation rentals. Consider how it will photograph. While this is true for *all* homes, in a vacation home, people are very often looking to get away from the chaos of their modern life. If their home is cluttered and messy with three kids and four pets, a serene, tidy, clutter-free Airbnb may be just what they want.

When people go to buy their family home, they try to picture their stuff in it. They look at the yard, the exterior, how many bedrooms, the floors and paint, and so on. But there's also a sense that if you don't like something, you can change it. Crisp gray walls might be popular, but maybe the buyer's daughter wants a lavender bedroom. It's a coat of paint.

When people choose a vacation home, they are picturing *themselves* there, not their stuff. Does it look relaxing? Clean? Welcoming? Will I really feel like I am getting away somewhere luxurious?

Ideally, you want the best photography. Even pay for a professional if you plan on making rentals a big part of your business model.

Social Media

Once upon a time, when you started a business, you incorporated, opened a bank account, found suitable office space, and worked up a marketing plan so people would know about you.

Today, with the internet, websites, social media platforms, and work-on-the-go or remote options, the business model has changed. Here are some top tips regarding your social media as a house flipper.

Start with Your Entity

As I have emphasized elsewhere in this book, I personally think your presence online and as a business should be the first thing you establish. If in the old days your storefront was the first thing people saw of your business, today your website is your so-called shingle.

As I said in **E: Entity,** try to consider your company names in terms of social media and online searches. For example:

Number One Realty

Number 1 Realty

No. 1 Realty

Home for You

Home 4 You

Home 4 U

There are so many ways to style things these days—especially as we add abbreviations through texting (such as *4 U*). So try to ensure your company name is spelled one way and one way only. I have a friend whose former boss's last name is one consonant and five vowels. Going by how it is pronounced would give you a completely different spelling on top of it. If you want to name your company after yourself, consider whether your last name is easy to remember or spell.

Also try to avoid things like this:

Home Magik

Home Magick

Clever or different spellings may get you a website if others are taken—but it won't make it any easier for Google (or clients) to find you.

Add Your Platforms

Choose the platforms that you are comfortable with—and that you will maintain. If you are a growing company, or, like me, branch into commercial development, you may at some point add staff who can handle your social media. But until that time, it's you.

What's worse—a company with just a website that doesn't use social, or a company with social media handles on four platforms—

that hasn't tweeted or been active since 2017? I personally think it's the latter, because in that case, it can be difficult to tell if the company is still in business.

The main platforms for businesses are as follows:

- LinkedIn

- Twitter (this is changing as the company changes under Elon Musk)

- Facebook

- Instagram

Instagram, because of its emphasis on photos and reels, is ideal for the photograph-heavy real estate market. People love viewing real estate.

LinkedIn is great for networking. Twitter is good for commentary on the real estate market itself or for brief promos. Facebook tends to be more personal—a way to interact directly with interested buyers, for example.

Here are a couple of tips for your social media campaigns:

- Use hashtags. Sometimes, it can look a little silly seeing twenty hashtags after an Instagram post. However, *that* is how you end up in searches. Here are some to try:

    #realestate
    #webuyhouses
    #webuyuglyhouses
    #houseflipping
    #houseflipper
    #houseflip
    #beforeandafter
    #renovation

#Reinvestor

#Reinvesting

#housesofinstagram

#houseflipsofinstagram

#cashbuyer

#houseforsale

#houseforsale[insert city or town here]

#househunting

#virtualhousetour

#virtualtour

- Join groups. You can find groups for real estate wholesalers, for every type of subcontractor, every type of investor, on Facebook. Use that to your advantage. Especially when new, be an active participant and forge relationships.

Get Real ... Reel

The current algorithms on social media favor video. Instagram has a stories feature—and you can save stories on your page in categories.

One reason to get real ... um ... reel ... besides the algorithm, is to get personal. No, I do not mean get on camera and complain about your personal life (you have a best friend for that). People tend to want to do business with someone they know, someone they feel they can trust. If you can relax on camera and speak about your flipped house, or show the progress on your flip, or anything having to do with your business that's of interest to home buyers while *also* allowing your personality to shine through, that's a win.

If you speak on camera, try to project being approachable and *caring*, and make it clear that you have a passion for your projects. Some people may try to do types of reels that could get a following, such as posting various real estate tips or DIY house projects. Rehabbing furniture is hot now, with people doing major transformations. So consider, too, whether there is something you can speak about consistently that you can post about.

Make Sure Your Content Is Professional

Ideally, you will become very capable at videotaping yourself or your houses or taking still photography. You want your pictures to look like the beautiful before-and-afters you see on Instagram or on television.

What can you post about?

Once you get started, you will be surprised at how you start looking at things visually and come up with content. Here are some ideas:

- Before-and-afters—room by room

- Pictures of a happy family you sold a house to, standing by the "Sold" sign

- Design concepts—for example, if the current hot trend is subway tile backsplashes or farmhouse sinks or glossy red doors, whatever it is, show it off if you are including that as part of your flip

- Your team (and we'll cover **T: Team** in the next letter)

- Cool touches of your staging

- Your specialty—if your company really excels at bathroom makeovers or backyard makeovers, show it off!

- Virtual tours

- Drone shots—many people *love* seeing a neighborhood and a house from up above

None of these will promote your business well if they aren't clear pictures with sharp colors. If you do not want to hire a professional photographer, consider investing in a good digital camera. If you do decide to hire a professional, find someone who specializes in real estate. It's tricky to photograph a room from the best angle to show its size.

And don't forget staging!

FLIP TIP

SOMETHING YOU MIGHT NOT THINK OF

I have one more social media tip for you. Social media is a way for buyers to find you. But it's *also* a way for you to find others. Use LinkedIn or Instagram or Facebook to reach out to the serious players in the real estate market where you live. Network, take them to coffee, or just introduce yourself.

Team

A house flipper's team is not small:

Wholesalers: Wholesalers are on the top of the list. Wholesalers develop a list of available properties they put under contract and resell very quickly. They usually only deal in distressed properties. But unlike flippers, they don't do any improvements to the property—just sell it to house flippers. In hot markets, wholesalers' inventories can go fast—so having a good relationship and networking with them is key.

REALTOR®, buying side: You need a REALTOR® who will help you buy properties. Ideally, you will work with someone who has experience with the unique needs of flippers. I mentioned elsewhere in the book that one time I worked with a buying-side REALTOR® who kept showing me properties that needed just a little work. In other words, they were at market value, and thus not right for a house flip. Needing a coat of paint in a living room or a little landscaping up front is not a true distressed property. (This assumes you do not have a REALTOR® license.)

REALTOR®, selling: On the other side of your house flip is a REALTOR® for the selling side. (Again, assuming you are not a licensed REALTOR®.) Ideally, they will have familiarity with house flipping. You want someone who understands the after-repair value and the way in which house flippers price their houses. You want someone who understands the value of the property. You should also look for someone with experience in the area. There is often a reason why in certain neighborhoods, you will see the same real estate agent's name on for sale signs—that agent may live in the neighborhood and know it well, or they may just have spent time getting to know it and thus understand the target market. Next, how is that agent going to market your property? Several times, in a hot market, my homes sold before I even stuck a sign in the yard. You don't want a REALTOR® who is simply going to list your home on the multiple listing service. What is their online presence? Do they do open houses? Do they mail postcards? Ask detailed questions of your potential REALTORS®.

Contractors, crews, subcontractors: without them, you can't do a flip.

Real estate attorney: Ideally, you will have a real estate attorney for advice on everything from real estate contracts to loans to agreements with management companies. After a while, you will become familiar with the clauses you need to look at—but it is always safest to have a good attorney with whom you have a relationship.

Contractors, crews, subcontractors: Without them, you can't do a flip. (Unless you are a contractor.) Finding reliable ones is a matter of both networking and establishing your credentials in the area you are working in. What sort of teams do you need? You sitting down?

- Carpenters

- Electricians

- Plumbers

- Roofers

- Installer, windows, doors

- Installer, floors

- Installer, garage door

- Installer, cabinets

- Tile workers

- Carpet layers

- Painters, inside

- Painters, outside

- Fencing installers

- Landscapers

- Security/alarm companies

- High-end finishers (if in that market)

- Driveway sealers

- Drywaller

- Pool repair company

- Inspectors (some of your general contractors offer this—you would rather know you have a problem *before* you have to close)

Home inspector: I sure as heck want to know if I set the thermostat at seventy-two in the heat of Austin whether the air coming out of the air conditioning registers is eighty-two or seventy-two degrees. A home inspector—a good one—can save you from the many uh-ohs that are often part of the home-buying and -flipping processes. The funny story of how we found ours happened when we were selling a house and the buyer's home inspector came in and found a few picky things that our own inspector had missed. I was grateful—I don't want to sell someone a house with something wrong; that would not have been good for our reputation, which we take pride in. So we turned around and hired that picky home inspector.

Accountant: Unless you very much know what you are doing, there are specific tax incentives, issues, and pitfalls of flipping houses. I wouldn't get too deep into house flipping as a business without an accountant. The bigger your company or business grows, the more important this is.

Architects: For some transformations to be successful, you must knock down a wall or open up a kitchen. You need an architect to make structural changes. Big open plans tend to be more popular because families like having the kitchen leading into the den so mom or dad can keep an eye on the kids while cooking. However, the global COVID-19 pandemic has led to some changes. Now with more remote work—and people remaining remote—they like being able to shut a door and set themselves apart from the household. It will be interesting to see how desires change. For now, an office space is a hot commodity.

Staging company: I know a couple of house flippers who maintain a warehouse for staging their flips. However, then you are paying for storage. And, frankly, just because you are a house flipper does not mean you know how to stage a house. Face it, we are not all experts in everything. Also, unless you are a medium-size to big operation, it's unlikely you have the choices in what you have as far as your staging inventory, as opposed to staging companies that do this all the time. Make sure your staging company is properly insured, as they will be having workers moving in and out of your property, and damage could happen. Also, you might consider looking for membership in RESA—the Real Estate Staging Association.

Lender, banker: You know, the money folks! You can't be in the flipping business without financing. Now, cash is king, and all-cash offers are a plus, but very few people are in that position, especially when you're just starting. It's also easier to be in this business if, like all these team members, you form a relationship with your lender or banker. House flippers are in a different position from home buyers who plan to buy and stay in their home a long time, not the least of which is wanting a short process time-wise.

Appraiser: Your buyer's lender will be basing their mortgage loan on the home's value. You can't have a $200,000 house and price it at $400,000 and think the buyer will be able to obtain a mortgage on it (I know that's obvious, but it's an easy example). If you examine my home inspection story earlier in the chapter, finding an appraiser who is the best and getting them to work with you is the goal.

Title insurance company: Most of the time, this is the seller's responsibility. Title insurance protects the buyer if it turns out the property has a lien on it or hasn't paid their property taxes (just two examples). Considering that distressed homes often have situations in which the owner has fallen behind on mortgage payments or the property has liens because the owner is in an unfortunate situation, it is especially important to have a good title insurance company as part of your team.

Assembling a *reliable* team is essential to your success.

Under Contract

Under contract—those are sweet words to a house flipper (even better is *Sold!*). As I've said throughout the book, you need to have your own real estate attorney. In addition, every state has its own regulations (just to make things complicated). But here are some basics.

What the Contract Should Have

Who: First, you will want the buyer's name, your company name, and signatures for both (no contract is valid without the signatures).

The property's information: For contracts, you need more than an address. Every property has a legal property description. The property will also have tax information (to track who pays the real estate taxes and that the money goes to the right place and property).

What's included, what's excluded: As I mentioned, every state has its own particular real estate laws. Generally, things that are included are the elements of a house that are truly attached to the home (such as outside light fixtures).

These are the common inclusions:

- Lighting fixtures (those screwed into ceilings or attached to the outside, sconces on walls, etc.)

- Landscaping

- Plumbing fixtures

- Garbage disposals

- Thermostats

- Ceiling fans

- Window treatments (these can also be *excluded*, so this is something to determine how you want to handle ahead of time)

- Hardware—cabinet drawer pulls, etc.

- Wall-to-wall carpeting

- Built-ins (shelving in a library or a built-in cupboard in a dining room, for example)

- Water softeners

- Automatic garage door equipment and remotes

- Kitchen appliances

- Washer and dryer

- Wine bar/fridge

Common exclusions include window treatments, some appliances, a Ring surveillance device (though usually a whole-home alarm system would stay).

Fees: This can be homeowner association fees (usually prorated, or the HOA asks for a year up front) or attorney fees. In some states, you do not need an attorney for real estate transactions (even though it is a good idea)—in those states it is not uncommon to have attorneys that offer closings at a flat fee.

Title insurance: Most of the time, this is the seller's responsibility. Title insurance protects the buyer if it turns out the property has a lien on it or hasn't paid their property taxes (just two examples). Considering that distressed homes often have situations in which the owner has fallen behind on mortgage payments or the property has liens because the owner is in an unfortunate situation, it is especially important to have a good title insurance company.

Real estate commission: If you have a REALTOR® license, you may save your seller's commission by handling it yourself. Otherwise, this is spelled out in the contract.

Warranty fees: Some homes come with a warranty. Home warranty companies charge a monthly fee for repairs to cover appliances, etc. in the home—they can cover appliances, air conditioning units, hot water heaters, and other big-ticket items that home buyers worry will break shortly after they move in and entail expenses they have not planned for.

Pest inspection: This is essential for a mortgage for the buyer and will be spelled out in the contract.

Closing costs: Not only will this be spelled out, but if the seller is paying some of the costs as a deal sweetener, that will be noted too.

Disclosures

If you know a home has a significant problem and you do not disclose it, you can find yourself being sued. While we all know the phrase *buyer beware*, the other side of the coin is that the seller must disclose defects. These disclosures can be things beyond the home, such as if a home is built close to a rifle range where gunshots can be heard all day long. Here are some examples of disclosures:

Someone died in the home: Now, we're not talking about an elderly person who passes away in their sleep. This disclosure would relate to a violent crime or something *property related*. (For example, if you had a pond on the property and a neighbor's child wandered over and drowned there, that would need disclosure.)

Neighborhood nuisances: This is like the rifle range I mentioned earlier (let me tell you, I have been in the backyard of someone with a beautiful home that was near a major army training base, and the helicopters flying overhead and the rat-a-tat-tat of gunfire was disconcerting). It could also be a farm with a slurry, a factory with extensive odors, etc. It also includes landfills, as well as being in an airport flight pattern.

Hazards: This includes radon, asbestos, and lead plumbing. These are chemicals and things that could directly harm people.

Repair history: This does not mean if you got your leaky faucet fixed. It is something structural that represents a major repair or potential problem. An example might be a foundation that needed to be repaired or if there was a major flood in the house that entailed extensive repairs to walls or floors.

Homeowner association: This is especially important to disclose if the homeowner association is getting ready to do a major assessment because they are not financially solvent, for example.

Water damage: We have all heard horror stories of toxic mold. If a home has had flooding, water retention in crawl spaces, roof leaks, or plumbing issues like pipes bursting inside a wall, this must be disclosed.

Termite damage: Enough said. What a nightmare.

Miscellaneous: Depending on your state, there could be other disclosures essential to make. For example, if an older home is part of the historic registry or if a city mandates that its repairs must be in line with historic standards.

Value

We've used the 70 Percent Rule a couple of times in this book because it is very important to a successful flip.

THE 70 PERCENT RULE

Most home flippers use the 70 Percent Rule to determine whether to purchase a home. This is the estimated value of the house after repairs are made as well as the estimated repair costs using this simple formula:

After-repair value (ARV) × 0.70 – Estimated repair costs = Maximum buying price

When analyzing a home to potentially buy, you are seeing if it will bring you the return you want. Here are some things to keep in mind:

The home will only increase to maximum value if you get all the repairs done. Be sure you have budgeted properly so you can complete all the projects needed. Your budget should have some wiggle room. That said, don't go down a rabbit hole of spending more and more for a home that may not get you that dollar value back. It's a fine line.

Don't fall in love with a house. Maybe you and your house-flipping partner walked into a house for sale at a low price. You fall in love with it—maybe you can envision the backyard space because there's a large oak tree there, or you know exactly how you would transform the interior space. Basic rule: don't fall in love. When you fall in love with a house, you can be blinded to its problems. Too many problems, and your ARV and repair costs can affect the bottom line.

Be objective. This goes hand in hand with the item above. Bring your contractor with you. Bring a checklist of things to look for. Don't get swayed into overpaying. See the repairs for what they are—remember, you make the most money when you flip *quickly*. The longer your flip takes, the less profit you will make. Therefore, especially for large-scale transformations, be sure you are clear eyed about what needs to be done.

Have a plan B. If you stay in this business long enough, it will happen. You will purchase a home and get in there, and it will become the proverbial money pit. I shared elsewhere in our alphabet that I rushed into purchasing a house because the market was so tight, and I thought my own inspection of it would be enough. I essentially made an offer on the spot. Then I discovered the foundation needed repairs. And, of course, I had bought it as a distressed property, as is. Plan B usually means getting out. Perhaps you don't do every renovation you planned—you just need to sell it before it eats even more of your budget.

Curb appeal. To get top dollar and value for your purchased flip home, don't discount what a difference curb appeal makes. A house with a new front door, window boxes or flowers or other tidy landscaping, a new mailbox, fresh exterior paint. You may need to reseed or resod a lawn. Don't leave it till it's punch-list time. Grass needs time to sprout and grow.

Outside space. When you purchase a flip home, pay attention to the backyard. In places with warm climates, outside space can be part of entertaining or family time 365 days a year. Even colder climates have months when a cozy backyard setting is everyone's favorite place to be.

Preforeclosures might be a deal. When looking for distressed properties, preforeclosures can be a good deal. You will likely get the house at a good price, and the seller may be inclined to move fast to avoid racking up more debt from missed mortgage payments.

Remember value is more than a house. While a house is usually people's biggest asset, the value of a home is more than the sum total of its parts. The schools, the neighborhood: these affect the perception of value buyers will have of your home. They are also things you have less control over—except when it comes to choosing the house. Make sure you evaluate the area well. Is there a grocery store nearby? A Target? Restaurants?

> **Remember value is more than a house.**

Dealbreakers. There are some elements (covered elsewhere in the book) that you should consider dealbreakers, such as foundation issues, mold issues, significant plumbing issues, and so on.

Not worth the money. Some things, such as a pool, generally do not add value to a house. Generally speaking, from my experiences, a pool is a top item that I don't think adds value. In fact, on distressed properties, very often they can have been neglected and hide significant problems. More than once, I have filled a pool in. Expensive finishes won't add to the value unless it's a high-end flip. Most people just want marble countertops. They won't appreciate a rare piece of marble imported from Italy. Drawer pulls should be sleek and functional—most buyers won't fully appreciate high-end drawer pulls inlaid with mother of pearl. This is not about *your* taste for the house you are going to live in for the next ten years. It's about fixing and flipping quickly.

Wholesalers

If you haven't picked up on it by reading this book or if you have skipped around on letters, for people who want to make house flipping their full-time business or an intensive side hustle, wholesalers are essential.

Here's a rundown of what they are all about.

Wholesalers sell in the short term. Basically, wholesalers make offers on multiple distressed houses. They snatch them up and then offer the contracts to house flippers.

Wholesalers charge a percentage for finding the property. Some charge 5 to 10 percent of the property's price.

Wholesalers' specialty is distressed homes.

EXAMPLE HOME WITH A WHOLESALER

A wholesaler comes upon a distressed home. An elderly man has passed away. His property had fallen into disrepair, and it is easily the most run-down house in a neighborhood with an excellent elementary school and attractive homes. The late homeowner's two daughters live in another state and really do not have the time or inclination to fix up the house. They list it for $120,000. Homes in that neighborhood start at $200,000. The wholesaler offers the daughters a quick sale at $100,000. Then the wholesaler finds an eager house-flipping investor and sells the contract for $125,000. The wholesaler pockets the difference, the seller got rid of it, and the house flipper plots how to renovate it and bring it up to market value.

Wholesalers will add you to their buyers list, which comes as an email blast, usually. You need to act quickly—especially in a hot sellers' market. It also pays—once again—to have a relationship with them. Seek them out at real estate networking events.

Remember they have distressed properties. Some wholesalers have better lists than others. Some will truly buy the most run-down properties there are. Be careful—which is why having an established relationship with them is so important.

eXpect the uneXpected

None of us like to think in the negative. But the fact is that house flipping is not like going and buying a pristine, just-built home, custom made for you. Whether you want to call it Murphy's Law or "eXpect the uneXpected," you need to be prepared.

One time, I bought a house where the wiring was particularly troublesome. Every time we thought we had it worked out, another light would blow. Our electricians handled it. But if you were doing the work yourself or hiring an hourly electrician, this is a kind of hiccup that can be frustrating.

Other times, the unexpected could be catastrophic. Discovering mold behind showers or that the foundation is sinking are not simply little fixes.

So without further ado, here are things to keep in mind when you expect that what can go wrong sometimes will go wrong:

Hire the best home inspector you can. One of the best ways to combat the unexpected is thorough due diligence. A home inspector can save you from a lot of heartache. Again, not everything that goes wrong will be a disaster, but you still can run into budget woes if you've planned for a bathroom remodel costing $2,000 but a mold issue means tearing out the shower wall and having to redo most of the bathroom, to the tune of double the allotted amount.

Ensure you have the right insurance. An on-the-job accident or other disasters mean you should have the right insurance for your house flip.

Blowing your budget. You must have a buffer. You cannot flip a home where you are literally making a budget down to your last one hundred dollars in the bank. This is too risky! Your budget has to have room for unexpected setbacks. *Do not underestimate your renovation costs.*

Plan for weather. Roofers can't put on a new roof in a hurricane. It's hard to do some work in Michigan in January. The weather is something you cannot control. Your schedule (and budget) should reflect wiggle room for those sorts of setbacks. Consider the weather where you live. There are going to be some months when buying (and selling) a home is easier.

Having to hold onto a house for longer than you intended. This could be because the renovation is taking longer than you expect. It could be because a house doesn't sell right away. I once did a flip that didn't sell initially—something so unusual for me. But then I decided to go ahead

and repaint the exterior to a better color. Just that, with new painted shutters, and a new painted door, and voilà! It sold the following weekend. At the time, I'd been flipping for a while and had more than one property, so I could absorb a little hiccup on one house. If you have put all your eggs in one basket on your first flip, having to hold a house longer than you planned can be stressful and eat into your budget (for example, you are paying a stager for the time the house is staged—and so every week longer you hold it, you are paying a company for the furniture and decor).

Contractor problems. If you are in the renovation business, you will have issues with contractors, subcontractors, and various companies you hire. It's part of the business. I have a friend whose final walk-through revealed the drywall team had done such a terrible, uneven job that one wall looked like there were waves at the top. Finding great people to work on your houses will be one of your biggest challenges. Not everyone takes pride in their work—and some contractors, depending on the employment market, are forced to hire day laborers who may be people who just want a paycheck.

The market. Ahh, the market. During the global COVID-19 pandemic, the market went a bit crazy in some areas—houses were being sold well above asking price. Then, interest rates were raised by the Fed, which led to a cooling down in some places. It's no wonder the ups and downs of the real estate market are enough to cause stress. But hopefully you are playing the long game. Expect the unexpected and plan.

Do not cut corners. Hire the cheapest contractor and you may pay for it later. This is where that budget needs to be

realistic. Otherwise, the unexpected may very well be shoddy work, or light fixtures that look horribly cheap.

Burglary and vandalism. This is another reason to have good insurance for your flip. If you are in this business long enough, you will eventually encounter this. Sadly, some people are simply dishonest. Burglary can be someone breaking in and stealing copper piping that you were storing in the garage (something they can sell) or one of your subcontractors stealing an expensive saw. Vandalism can be teens breaking in to have a house party or to vandalize for the sake of vandalizing with graffiti or worse. I shared elsewhere about a friend's parents set to close in days on a 5,000-plus-square-foot house in a tony area of Manhattan's suburbs when delinquent teens broke in and set a fire. The closing ended up delayed for seven weeks. Vandalism on your job site can set you back. One way of combating this is ensuring you introduce yourself to the neighbors and asking them to keep an eye. Most neighborhoods are very happy when a distressed home or an eyesore is finally being updated and repaired. It only helps the value of their home. Some sites will install cameras.

It's your house until closing. By the time you are nearly done and closing is a week or two away, it's very tempting to breathe easy. But truly, you are carrying that house until you sign the closing papers. Anything can go wrong, from a title search turning something up, to burst pipes, to … you name it. Stay vigilant on all the things you need to in order to ensure the house goes to closing as planned.

Code compliance. I know another real estate tale that illustrates expecting the unexpected. If you have great contractors, hopefully everything is to code. But I know of a house where the sellers had bought the home five years before—and a pool and back deck were already done. They closed. No one raised any issues. But then the house flipper bought the property—and the county discovered, via a neighbor complaint, that the pool deck was four inches too close to the neighbor's property line. *Four inches!* Entailing—you guess it—having to redo it.

I heard a flipper horror story where they bought a distressed house, laid down all new floor, new siding, etc. However, it turned out the previous owners were drug dealers (it was a foreclosure). This meant unsavory people were turning up at the job site often, looking for the previous owners. Concerned about safety, the flipper added better locks, a Ring security device, huge outside lights for nighttime, and other measures to ensure the message got out this was now a respectable home in a decent neighborhood.

The bottom line is if you go into real estate in general, and house flipping in particular, there will be stories. "That time I bought this house and …" It's part of the business. The problem is if you are not prepared with your budget, time, or proactive actions (such as guarding against theft), your profit and business will suffer.

You!

I knew when I first sat down to write this book that *Y* was going to be *you*! Because you will help determine whether your house flip will be successful or not.

Before you enter the house-flipping market, ask yourself these questions:

How will you locate properties?

Are you networking already?

What work do you plan on doing yourself?

Do you have your team ready? Remember, speed is of the essence in a house flip. As soon as the ink is dry on your purchase of the house, you should already have people at the ready. *After* you've bought is too late to go on Yelp and try to find an electrician. In hot markets, it's even less likely you will find qualified people who are available.

Are you ready to juggle all the different elements of a house flip? This is why partnering for the first one can be a positive thing. As is often said, "You don't know what you don't know." You can prepare and read books like this one or google the heck out of "how to flip a house," but there will still be threads of the job that you have to learn. And that first home can be a steep learning curve.

Can you be objective and not jump at houses that are going to cost too much or demand too much in renovations? Don't think like a home buyer. Think like an investor. Think like a businessperson.

Can you take the risk? Most likely, unless you are flipping with a partner's money, you are going to have skin in the game. Be sure you can take the risk—especially since budgets can easily run off course.

Network. Talk to other flippers. Be sure you have appropriate expectations.

Do you have a realistic view of what house flipping will be like? Please do not get all your inspiration from HGTV and renovation shows. They are heavily edited; the people who star on them have usually been doing it a long time—and have deep pockets to carry the risk. The shows depict setbacks sometimes. ("When we knocked down this wall, we weren't expecting to see that the wiring was not up to code.") However, those all have to be resolved in an hour of TV (including commercials). Network. Talk to other flippers. Be sure you have appropriate expectations.

Success Principles

The flipping side of the business aside, you also need to bring success principles to your business. Here are just a few that I think are important to being a successful house flipper and real estate investor:

1. **Be professional.** Call people when you say you are going to call. Be on time (otherwise, how can you ask your team to be timely?). Respect your team.

2. **Set goals.** When I first started flipping houses, I had a goal of flipping two houses by a set date. Having that goal in mind helped me stay focused and not get discouraged. After I surpassed my goal many times over, I set a goal to get involved in business investments—and now I have achieved that as well.

3. **Surround yourself with smart people.** I am book smart— but also through this business, I've become construction smart. Know your weak spots, and find people you can learn from. Different people are smart in different ways. You may not be capable of rewiring a kitchen—but you should have a great electrician team who can.

4. **Keep learning.** This is a learning business. Every single house flip is different. I feel like I should shout that from the rooftops. They all have their own unique challenges and triumphs. Stay curious about this business you are in, and keep learning about it every day.

5. **Take care of yourself.** This is a business with very long days. Work crews can start as the sun is rising, and there can be calls and administrative duties going on well into the evening hours, not to mention keeping track of expenses and spreadsheets … and … and. Take care of yourself with enough rest, healthy lifestyle, and so on.

6. **Plan every day.** This is a business with many moving parts. If you are not a meticulous planner, you can find yourself

pulled in a dozen directions—and performing poorly in each. Manage your own time carefully.

7. **Be organized.** Sometimes I think a house flip is like one of those math problems we had in grade school. You know the ones: "If Tom has a work crew of four roofers but only two show up, and Sam has misordered the tiles so that there are only 2,500 but the roof needs 3,700, how many days will it take for the new roof to go up?" There are so many moving parts, and it's essential that you be organized to achieve success.

8. **Stay positive.** Success breeds success. A successful mindset grows success. There will probably be days when you will question why it is you ever decided to flip houses in the first place. But whatever mindfulness you practice, stay positive and forward looking.

9. **Have integrity.** I always knew my homes were built well and that our whole team gave their all. I never cut corners because I intended to be in real estate investment for a long time. I wanted my word to count. I wanted my homes to stand tall and proud. I wanted people to return to me the next time they wanted to buy a house and say, "I want to work with you again."

10. **Go the extra mile.** Again, my reputation must stand on its own. That means going the extra mile for my clients. As an investor now, I apply that same mindset.

11. **Communicate effectively.** Mistakes happen on job sites or in the budget when people do not communicate clearly. This is not a job for timid people (unless you have a partner

with a strong personality). You will be working with all sorts of job crews. Also, that is difficult at times for women in a male-dominated business. I always worked to communicate firmly, clearly, and in a way that ensured there were no misunderstandings.

12. **Teamwork.** Without teams, you cannot flip houses. It's that simple. Ideally, you can assemble a team that functions—no one wants a toxic workplace with crews shouting at each other and you shouting at them. Cultivate teamwork through respect and fairness.

13. **Have a big picture dream.** If your dreams don't scare you a little, they are probably too small.

Finally, before you even start flipping houses, sit down and write *why*. What about this business fascinates you? Why do you find it exciting? What is your big dream? Tuck that slip of paper in your wallet for days when the coffee machine breaks and the cabinets were mismeasured. Remind yourself why you are doing this.

Zoos!

Yes, the letter *Z* was difficult. So I settled on "Zoos." But zoos are a metaphor here for what is around a community that attracts families and couples and home buyers of every sort.

We're back to our motto of *location, location, location.* Zoos, for this chapter, are about community and what people look for when choosing where to live.

Many people flip houses where they live or nearby. They know the community. But I know there are people (myself included) who have flipped houses in places not near them. Either way, it's important to evaluate the community. Here are some things people look for when choosing a place to buy a home.

1. **Walkability score.** To some people, this is very important. They like living in a walkable community. Bike paths and

sidewalks also affect the walkability score (there are online tools that help you evaluate a community's walkability).

2. **Commuting ease.** While more people are working from home than ever before, many people have returned to the office, and some are doing a hybrid office situation. If there are big companies around, there will be people needing to commute there. Is there public transportation? Is downtown a congested mess? Does traffic make driving in your own town near five o'clock utterly impossible?

3. **Crime rates.** People want to live in a safe community. Crime rates definitely affect the decisions of home buyers.

4. **Green space, parks (and zoos!).** People seek out places with green space, parks, bike paths, places to get fresh air and exercise. Those with children like seeing parks and baseball diamonds and places where children can play.

5. **Housing costs.** While this may seem obvious, in fact, people may avoid places that are just becoming too expensive. An interesting phenomenon during COVID-19 was people moving away from expensive cities like New York and renting or buying in cheaper areas where their money goes further.

6. **Grocery stores and necessities.** I have a friend who lived in an urban area in a great apartment, but the city was a food desert, except for bodegas. To buy groceries, she had to drive twenty-five minutes to the next town over—and it was twenty-five unpleasant minutes with run-down roads and potholes. Grocery stores, medical offices, stores like Target, and so on are basic necessities for people.

7. **Entertaining and dining.** People work hard—and then they like to play. Is your community a foodie town? Are there many dining options—both for families and for more adult evenings out? What about nightlife? Live music, theaters, festivals: these are all things that can make a city or town appealing.

8. **Culture.** People often cite wanting culture around where they live. This usually means museums, plays, and other events and places to enrich their lives.

9. **Diversity.** Many people want to know how diverse a city is. They enjoy being around a variety of different people and cultures; they want their children to grow up accepting of other people and cultures. If they are from a diverse culture, they may want to know there are other people there who share that culture so they feel less isolated. This even plays into restaurants—Austin, New York City, Seattle, and Miami, for example, are foodie paradises with cuisine from every culture.

10. **Climate.** For some, climate will factor into their choices. Some people want the temperate climate of Southern California. Others want to ski in Denver.

11. **Sports.** For sports lovers, are there teams to root for and games to go to? Does the city have a minor league baseball team or a college team to root for in basketball?

12. **Churches, temples, and spiritual places.** For many people, as soon as they move somewhere, they want to try different churches, temples, or other spiritual community gathering places to pick one that suits them. Are there a variety of

denominations? Are churches and temples and other houses of worship part of the community?

13. **Hospitals and medical offices.** For some people, having a respected hospital or being near top doctors is important. This will be especially true for people suffering from chronic conditions or who are aging and concerned about that in the future.

14. **The vibe and the people.** Most people want to live in a place where they can make friends. Every community has a vibe. Some are more welcoming than others.

15. **Employment opportunities.** Most people want to know that if they leave their current job, there is more than one employer in town (this was something that got more attention when auto companies would shut plants, for example, and there was nowhere else for the laid-off people to work nearby). They want to know opportunities are there for them, their partner, and eventually their children.

AFTER THE ALPHABET

Some Final Words

I hope you have enjoyed our trip through the alphabet and the ABCs of flipping and renovation. No single book could encompass all the ins and outs of this fascinating business, but I hope my book has given you an idea of what is involved—and that you use this book as a resource throughout your career.

House flipping has and always will have a special place in my heart. That's how API started, and that was my first business concept here in the United States. And, in my opinion, we did quite well. House renovations gave us a great start and allowed us to grow the company and move onto other interests and larger possibilities.

I personally think we at API were truly blessed, even though some may say when we were starting that the times were unclear and unpredictable. But you have to take risks. We did, and it has paid off. API is growing as a company, and now our main focus is business acquisition. You may think it's a jump and that flipping houses and acquiring businesses are way too far apart; I think flipping gave us a great foundation and capital, which allowed us to grow.

We all come from different cities, states, and even countries. We may believe in different things, but business principles stay pretty similar—it doesn't matter where you are. I hope this book was useful to you, dear reader. Use it as a guide. It's not a book you read one time and forget about; with this book you can always come back and find the letter you need, and there you are, reading about finances or home design.

So here's to you, my readers. Happy flipping!

ACKNOWLEDGMENTS

Writing a book is harder than I thought and more rewarding than I could have ever imagined.

None of this would be possible without my best friend and husband, Andy. He stood by me during every struggle and all my success. That is more than marriage; that is friendship.

He saw a woman in me who was hungry to learn, hungry to grow, and hungry to succeed in business. He never stopped me; he only encouraged me.

I'm eternally grateful to my dear parents, who were always there for me. They taught me discipline, love, manners, respect, and so much more that helped me to succeed in life.

To my kids, who teach me every day how to be a better human, who gave me a chance to be a mom.

This book reflects my first steps in business. And though it's a hard but surreal process, it would not be possible without those special people in my life.

To the editorial team and publisher that took a chance on me, knowing this was my very first book, and saw potential. Thank you for believing in me.

I want to thank God most of all. He has given me strength and encouragement throughout all the challenging moments of completing this book. I am truly grateful for his unconditional and endless love, mercy, and grace.

ABOUT THE AUTHOR

Afa Pitts is a real estate developer and founder of API Inc. based in Austin, Texas. She is involved in a wide variety of projects and investments throughout the Southwest. With a background in medicine, and a keen entrepreneurial eye, Afa has focused her creative talents and managerial and business acumen toward real estate.

As a woman business leader, she has been a force to reckon with, using her drive to find opportunities in one of the hottest real estate development markets in the United States. Though API has expanded into business acquisition, Afa still regularly shares her insights and guidance in the house flipping arena. Now, at last, she has assembled her best advice into one comprehensive book.

ENDNOTES

1 Mark Ferguson, "Can You Make $1 Million a Year Flipping Houses?" accessed May 4, 2022, https://www.forbes.com/sites/forbesrealestatecouncil/2019/08/20/can-you-make-1-million-a-year-flipping-houses/?sh=737977784719.

2 Nadia Evangelou, "How Long Do Homeowners Stay in Their Homes?" January 8, 2020, https://www.nar.realtor/blogs/economists-outlook/how-long-do-homeowners-stay-in-their-homes#:~:text=As%20of%202018%2C%20the%20median,varies%20from%20area%20to%20area.

3 Darcy Sprague and Amy Denney, "Austin Named Second-Fastest-Growing Major City in Texas, Adding about 171,000 Residents from 2010-20," January 27, 2022, https://communityimpact.com/austin/northwest-austin/data-reference/2022/01/27/austin-named-second-fastest-growing-major-city-in-texas-adding-about-171000-res-idents-from-2010-20/#:~:text=The%20city%20of%20Austin%20grew,44%25%20growth%20in%20Williamson%20County.

4 US Bureau of Labor Statistics, "Real Estate Brokers and Sales Agents," Occupational Outlook Handbook, accessed May 8, 2022, https://www.bls.gov/ooh/sales/real-estate-brokers-and-sales-agents.htm#:~:text=in%20May%202021.-,Job%20Outlook,on%20average%2C%20over%20the%20decade.

5   C. B. Frey and M. A. Osborne, "The Future of Employment: How Susceptible Are Jobs to Computerisation?" September 17, 2023, https://www.oxfordmartin.ox.ac.uk/downloads/academic/The_Future_of_Employment.pdf.

6   "How to Choose the Right Real Estate Agent," Zillow, accessed May 11, 2022, https://www.zillow.com/sellers-guide/choose-right-real-estate-agent/.

7   "Real Estate Investing (REI) Certification," National Association of REALTORS®, accessed May 12, 2022, https://www.nar.realtor/designations-and-certifications/real-estate-investing-rei.

8   "Dog Ownership Statistics," Spirit Dog Training, accessed May 11, 2022, https://spiritdogtraining.com/dog-ownership-statistics-usa/#:~:text=We%20surveyed%202%2C000%20US%20residents,own%20more%20than%20one%20dog.

9   "2022 Most Popular Décor Trends by State," Living Spaces, accessed May 28, 2022, https://www.livingspaces.com/inspiration/ideas-advice/styles/most-popular-decor-trends-by-state.

10 "Expert Tax Strategies for Flipping Houses," We Lend, September 18, 2020, https://www.welendllc.com/blog/expert-tax-strategies-for-flipping-houses#:~:text=The%20standard%20tax%20consequences%20of,profit%20as%20'normal%20income.

11 "Flipping Houses and Mortgage Loan Fraud," HG.org, accessed May 29, 2022, https://www.hg.org/legal-articles/flipping-houses-and-mortgage-loan-fraud-48379.

12 Will Kenton, "Brand," Investopedia, updated March 24, 2022, https://www.investopedia.com/terms/b/brand.asp.

13 Shonda Novak, "Amid Pandemic, Foreign Buyers Spent $624 Million on Austin-Area Properties, Report Finds," *Austin American-Statesman*, October 27, 2021, https://www.statesman.com/story/business/real-

estate/2021/10/27/foreign-buyers-spent-634-million-austin-area-properties-amid-pandemic/8551690002/.

14 Audrey McGlinchy, "Trying to Buy a Home in Austin? So Are Investors," KUT.org, February 8, 2022, https://www.kut.org/austin/2022-02-08/trying-to-buy-a-home-in-austin-so-are-investors.

15 Justin Pritchard, "Types of Loans for Flipping Houses," The Balance, updated February 13, 2022, https://www.thebalance.com/loans-for-flipping-houses-4129189#:~:text=It%20is%20possible%20to%20use,cash%20for%20a%20down%20payment.

16 Dan Mihalascu, "Tesla Investing $10 Billion in Giga Austin, Will Create 20,000 Jobs," Inside EVs, December 17, 2021, https://insideevs.com/news/555221/tesla-investing-10billion-giga-texas/.

17 Peter Warden, "Home Inspection Checklist: What Do Home Inspectors Look For?," The Mortgage Reports, April 5, 2022, https://themortgagereports.com/37715/home-inspection-checklist-what-to-expect-on-inspection-day.

18 "About Audience Targeting," Google Ads Help, January 5, 2023, https://support.google.com/google-ads/answer/2497941?hl=en.

19 "When Is Peak Moving Season?" MovingLabor.com, November 27, 2022, https://help.movinglabor.com/start/peak-moving-season.

20 MovingLabor.com, "When Is Peak Moving Season?"

21 Vishal Sanjay, "Top 5 Best QuickBooks Alternatives," Business News Daily, updated September 16, 2022, https://www.businessnewsdaily.com/16240-quickbooks-alternatives.html.

22 Maya Kosoff, "LinkedIn Just Bought Online Learning Company Lynda for $1.5 Billion," Insider, April 9, 2015, https://www.businessinsider.com/linkedin-buys-lyndacom-for-15-billion-2015-4.

23   Sara Coleman, "The Cost of Owning a Pet in 2022," Bankrate.
com, March 31, 2022, https://www.bankrate.com/insurance/home-
owners-insurance/pet-ownership-cost-statistics/#:~:text=Pet%20
ownership%20statistics,-Pet%20ownership%20statistics&text=A%20
2021%2D2022%20survey%20conducted,households%20that%20
own%20a%20cat.

24   "The Best Urban Airbnb Markets in the USA," HostAway.
com, accessed August 14, 2022, https://www.hostaway.com/
the-best-urban-airbnb-markets-in-the-usa/.

25   "Best Places to Invest in Vacation Rentals," AirDNA.com, accessed
August 10, 2022, https://www.airdna.co/best-places-to-invest-in-
vacation-rentals?utm_term=&utm_campaign=PMAX_Income&utm_
source=google&utm_medium=cpc&hsa_acc=6167315757&hsa_
cam=16380170594&hsa_grp=&hsa_ad=&hsa_src=x&hsa_tgt=&hsa_
kw=&hsa_mt=&hsa_net=adwords&hsa_ver=3&gclid=Cj0KCQjwj7C
ZBhDHARIsAPPWv3dJrumuqXQo6p-O5FpDmEfJcyEQWD8oX-
hofCgSSlZHqG1CBM-53_b0aAiLwEALw_wcB.